RESCUING THE REVOLUTION

Unsung Patriot Heroes and the Ten Crucial Days
of
America's War for Independence

David Price

Historical Interpreter
Washington Crossing Historic Park

A Note About the Cover

The image shown on the cover is that of the Continental Army soldiers marching to Trenton, New Jersey in the early morning hours of December 26, 1776 after their fabled crossing of the Delaware River, as portrayed by Don Troiani in his 2014 painting entitled "Victory or Death." The title of the painting is based upon the password devised by George Washington for the plan to cross the river and attack the Hessian brigade occupying Trenton.

Other Books by Author David Price

The Road to Assunpink Creek: Liberty's Desperate Hour and the Ten Crucial Days of the American Revolution

John Haslet's World: An Ardent Patriot, the Delaware Blues, and the Spirit of 1776

The Battle of Harlem Heights, 1776

A Note About Terminology

As used in this narrative, the term "patriot" is meant to connote active support for, or at a minimum sympathy with, the effort made by the 13 American colonies to secure their independence from Great Britain during the American Revolution, and the term "loyalist" is meant to connote opposition to that effort based upon a desire to maintain the colonies' status within the British Empire as entities subject to the authority of the British Crown and Parliament. American patriots were sometimes referred to as Whigs and loyalists as Tories in reference to the different political factions in Britain.

To

Alison, Madeline, Gwyneth,

and the Friends of Washington Crossing Park

I love the man that can smile in trouble, that can gather strength from distress, and grow brave by reflection.

> \- Thomas Paine, from *The American Crisis*,
> Number I, 19 December 1776

It is not in the still calm of life, or the repose of a pacific station, that great characters are formed. The habits of a vigorous mind are formed in contending with difficulties. Great necessities call out great virtues. When a mind is raised, and animated by scenes that engage the heart, then those qualities which would otherwise lay dormant, wake into life and form the character of the hero and the statesman.

> \- Abigail Adams, from a letter to her son,
> John Quincy Adams, 19 January 1780

I am aware that a man of real merit is never seen in so favourable a light as seen through the medium of adversity. The clouds that surround him are shades that set off his good qualities.

> \- Lt. Col. Alexander Hamilton, from a letter
> to Lt. Col. John Laurens, 11 October 1780

Contents

Preface

The victories achieved by the American cause during the "Ten Crucial Days" of our war for independence from Great Britain were the product of bold and imaginative leadership on the part of George Washington and his fellow generals, miscalculation by the enemy, and the fortuitous effects of weather as it related to the movement of troops and battlefield conditions. But those storied triumphs were also due to the heroic feats of people less well known to history who remain the "unsung heroes" behind our nation's struggle for independence during its darkest days.

What follows is an attempt to convey the significance of their actions during perhaps the most critical few days in the history of our country by highlighting the efforts of several such individuals. They represent just a few of the unrecognized heroes of that period and only a handful of the many who joined in the revolutionary cause and in some cases gave to it what Lincoln would have termed "their last full measure of devotion."

I chose to write about these individuals because I find their stories especially compelling and hope that the reader will as well. The intent of this project was to cover a small but representative sample of the actors who made important contributions in relation to the military events of this period and in some cases beyond it. In doing so, I took into account their varying backgrounds, ages, places of residence, and wartime exploits. The stories of their deeds are intertwined within the larger narrative of how the Continental Army narrowly escaped destruction in the waning days of 1776 and set America on the road to eventual victory against the vaunted might of the British Empire.

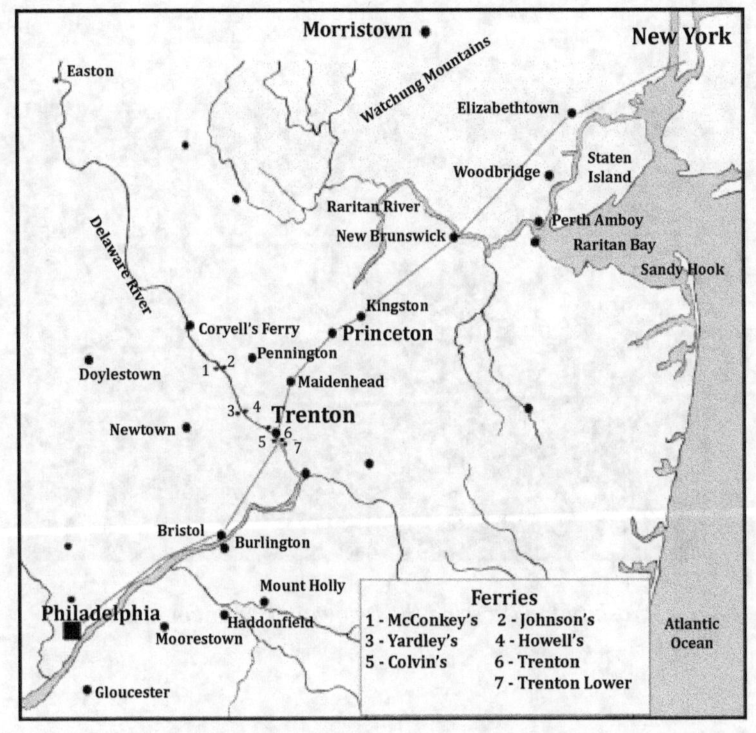

Central New Jersey: 1776-1777

Washington Crossing the Delaware (Emanuel Leutze)

Chapter 1

From Defeat to Defiance

I cannot help being astonished that a people should come three thousand miles at so much risk, trouble, and expense to rob, plunder, and destroy ... because [another people] will not lay their lives and fortunes at their feet.
- Col. Joseph Reed, Adjutant General of the Continental Army, from a letter to his wife, Esther, 9 August 1776

The period that historians have dubbed the "Ten Crucial Days" of the American Revolution - from 25 December 1776 through 3 January 1777 - marked a defining moment in our nation's struggle for independence. During that span of time, the Continental Army, under the command of Gen. George Washington, won its first three significant victories against the British and their German allies - the latter then collectively known to us as "Hessians"[1] - and reversed the momentum of the contest. Just when it appeared that Washington's force was on the verge of collapse and quite possibly the Revolution with it, the American forces ignited their legendary comeback.

In December 1776, the fate of the new American nation was very much in doubt, even though the Continental Congress had declared that infant country's independence from Great Britain six months earlier. The Continental Army had lost every significant battle that it had fought against the enemy, beginning in the preceding summer - at Long Island in August, Kip's Bay in September, White Plains in October, and Fort Washington in November - and had been driven out of New York and across New Jersey into Pennsylvania. The army had dwindled to about ten percent of its original strength due to battlefield casualties, disease, desertions, and expired enlistments. "In just three months," according to one tally, "the British had taken 4,500 prisoners and almost 3,000 muskets along with close to 250 cannons and 17,000 cannonballs."[2] Many of Washington's remaining soldiers were expected to leave the ranks when

---

[1]The princes of seven German provinces hired out troops to fight for Great Britain during the war, and about two-thirds of those who served in America came from the provinces of Hesse-Cassel and Hesse-Hanau. Technically, only the latter were "Hessians," but Americans generally referred to all the German soldiers by that name. Contrary to popular belief, they were not "mercenaries" because Britain was paying each prince for his soldiers' services, rather than the soldiers themselves, although the latter were in each case generally well compensated by their prince for their service.

[2]Nathaniel Philbrick, *Valiant Ambition: George Washington, Benedict Arnold, and the Fate of the American Revolution* (New York: Viking, 2016), 61.

their one-year enlistments expired on 31 December unless their commanding general could somehow contrive to alter the fortunes of his army before that date.

At the beginning of 1776, an American invasion of Canada, with a view to making it the 14th colony, had ended in ignominious defeat when an army under Richard Montgomery and Benedict Arnold was routed in the snows of Quebec. The threat of an enemy thrust down the Hudson River from Canada to link up with the occupying British force in New York was ever present, threatening to cut New England off from the rest of the continent to her south. Moreover, the British had seized Rhode Island virtually without a shot in the aftermath of their triumphant New York campaign.

By December 1776, the Continental Congress had fled from Philadelphia to Baltimore in anticipation of an enemy attack, and the army's most experienced senior officer, Gen. Charles Lee, had been captured by the British in what was then regarded as a severe blow to the patriot cause. Concerns about Washington's leadership and judgment were beginning to circulate among some of his own officers and in the Continental Congress. Moreover, many of his soldiers lacked such basic items as winter clothing, shoes, stockings, and blankets. British military leadership believed that American resistance was on the verge of crumbling, as reflected in Capt. Francis Lord Rawdon's observation that "their army is broken all to pieces" and "it is well nigh over with them."[3]

---

[3]David McCullough, *1776* (New York: Simon & Schuster, 2005), 251.

It appeared to many that the long chain of events dating back to 1765, which had led to open rebellion by the 13 colonies against the mother country, was about to end with the collapse of organized resistance by those rebellious American subjects. If so, Britain would achieve by its military prowess what it had been unable to through its colonial laws and regulations during the prior decade - to make America resemble the Ireland of that period, "a conquered dominion where, although the inhabitants had their own laws and their own peculiar faith, everyone knew where authority ultimately lay."[4] This would be the decisive end to a struggle that British Prime Minister Lord North later termed a war to maintain "the just rights of parliament, or in other words, of the people of Great Britain, over the dependencies of the empire."[5]

After funding a series of expensive wars in Europe and North America, the British Parliament had made repeated attempts to impose taxes on the colonists, which were bitterly and sometimes violently opposed, beginning with the Stamp Act of 1765. Parliament asserted its right to impose such policies upon the colonies as it deemed necessary through the Declaratory Act of 1766. The ensuing protest and retribution took many forms: the "Boston Massacre" committed by occupying British soldiers in March 1770; the colonists' dumping of East

---

[4]Nick Bunker, *An Empire on the Edge: How Britain Came to Fight America* (New York: Alfred A. Knopf, 2014), 18.

[5]Eric Nelson, *The Royalist Revolution: Monarchy and the American Founding* (Cambridge, MA: The Belknap Press of Harvard University Press, 2014), 4.

India Company tea into Boston Harbor in December 1773 in protest of the British tax on tea; the adoption of a series of punitive measures by Parliament in retaliation for the "Boston Tea Party," which included the occupation of Boston by British troops who replaced those withdrawn after the Boston Massacre; and the convening of a first Continental Congress in September 1774 and a second in May 1775 to formulate the colonies' unified response to British policy.

Debate eventually turned to battle when occupying redcoats and an aroused American militia fired upon each other at Lexington and Concord on 19 April 1775. In June 1775, the Continental Army was formed with George Washington as its commander-in-chief after the pyrrhic British victory in the slaughter at Bunker Hill. In August, King George III issued a proclamation declaring the colonies to be in a state of rebellion, and that rebellion gave rise to the siege of Boston by the Continental Army that forced British evacuation in March 1776. The colonies formally severed their connection to the United Kingdom in July, by which time Britain had dispatched the largest invasion force that ever sailed from the Old World to the New, with the intent of crushing the American rebellion in one devastating blow. After the rout of Washington's troops in the New York campaign, the British pursued the colonials across New Jersey in late fall while the latter desperately sought to elude their British and Hessian pursuers and seek safety in Pennsylvania. As the Americans made their way across the Delaware River during the first week of December, those "on the last boat to leave swore they could hear the music of British fifes and drums."[6]

By December 1776, it appeared as if the drama was almost played out, with the remnants of Washington's bruised and battered army on one side of the Delaware River and their adversary firmly ensconced on the other. On 30 November, Gen. William Howe, commander-in-chief of the British Army in North America, and his brother, Adm. Richard Lord Howe, issued a proclamation offering amnesty to any colonist willing to swear allegiance to the Crown within the following 60 days, and at least 3,000 people would take them up on their offer. Frustrated by the difficulties encountered in finding reinforcements for his rapidly dwindling force, Washington confided in a letter to his brother, Augustine, on December 18: "If every nerve is not strained to recruit a new Army with all possible expedition, I think the game is pretty near up."[7]

Fortunately for the American cause, the British had left themselves open to attack by spreading out their forces in New Jersey along a line of garrison posts that extended from Perth Amboy to the banks of the Delaware River, with the most vulnerable being the Hessian force of 1,500 soldiers commanded by Col. Johann Rall in Trenton. Gen. Howe remained confident that the Continental Army would soon wither away and so tempted fate by this

---

[6]Frank Dale, *Delaware Diary: Episodes in the Life of a River* (New Brunswick, NJ: Rutgers University Press, 1996), 35.

[7]David Hackett Fischer, *Washington's Crossing* (New York: Oxford University Press, 2004), 151.

geographic dispersion of his troops; however, he "simply did not have enough soldiers to occupy what land he had so far secured and wage a proper war against the Americans."[8] Moreover, he proved to be a victim of his own success by driving his opponent to pursue a do-or-die undertaking that Howe never envisioned.[9] Washington, desperate to save his army and the patriot cause, would launch the weary but determined patriot warriors across a swollen, ice-laden river and lead them through a blizzard to strike the sleeping enemy in Trenton.

The ensuing chain of events resulted in three American victories that turned the tide of the war - the First Battle of Trenton against the Hessian Brigade under Col. Rall on 26 December 1776; the Second Battle of Trenton (sometimes referred to as the Battle of Assunpink Creek) against a British and Hessian force under Gen. Charles Cornwallis on 2 January 1777; and the Battle of Princeton against a small British force under Lt. Col. Charles Mawhood on 3 January 1777. These wins compelled the British and Hessians to vacate most of New Jersey and cost them dearly in terms of casualties, lost weapons, and supplies. They also shattered the illusion of British and Hessian invincibility and dampened enemy spirits. At the same time, these events bolstered American morale and encouraged new enlistments in the Continental Army. This

---

[8]Philbrick, 64.

[9]Andrew Jackson O'Shaughnessy, *The Men Who Lost America: British Leadership, the American Revolution, and the Fate of the Empire* (New Haven, CT: Yale University Press, 2013), 101.

string of victories also helped prompt the French, who were providing covert assistance to America in the form of arms and ammunition, to seriously consider a formal alliance with the new nation.

The rapid-fire colonial triumphs largely altered the public perception of Washington as well and dramatically enhanced his stature as a heroic figure and stalwart symbol of what he termed the "glorious cause" - meaning the defense of American liberty.[10] During this period, Abigail Adams wrote to her husband, John, then a delegate to the Continental Congress (and the future first Vice President and second President of the United States): "I am apt to think that our late misfortunes have called out the hidden excellencies of our commander-in-chief." [11]

The British were now forced to adopt a newfound, if grudging, respect for the fighting capacity of American soldiers. "Though it was once the fashion of this army to treat them in the most contemptible light," Col. William Harcourt would write his father in March 1777, "they are now become a formidable enemy."[12]

As the new year 1777 dawned, it was apparent that the quest for independence had new life and that the supporters of American independence felt a renewed

---

[10]Robert Middlekauff, *The Glorious Cause: The American Revolution, 1763-1789* (New York: Oxford University Press, 2005), 302.

[11]David McCullough, *John Adams* (New York: Simon & Schuster, 2001), 168.

[12]Henry Steel Commager and Richard B. Morris, eds., *The Spirit of 'Seventy-Six: The Story of the American Revolution as Told by Participants* (New York: Harper & Row, Publishers, 1967), 524.

optimism about its prospects for success. As one account reminds us, "Superstitious folk had feared the coming of 1777, for the numerals resembled a gallows: Rebels would hang that year. But suddenly the gallows seemed remote."[13]

The battles at Trenton and Princeton were transformational events in the Revolutionary War and, as such, could lay plausible claim to being the most important ever fought by American soldiers. It has been argued that no other battle in the Revolution was "more important in overall terms (politically, morally, and psychologically)" than the clash with the Hessians along the banks of the Delaware River on 26 December.[14]

Lord George Germain, Britain's Secretary of State for North America and principal architect of his government's military strategy for winning the war, later lamented in a speech to Parliament: "all our hopes were blasted by that unhappy affair at Trenton."[15] Ironically enough, it was another Englishman, Sir George Otto Trevelyan, who perhaps most succinctly and eloquently summarized the significance of the events during this period when he wrote, more than a century later in an acclaimed history of the Revolution: "It may be doubted whether so small

---

[13]Bart McDowell, *The Revolutionary War* (Washington, DC: National Geographic Society, 1967), 109.

[14]Phillip Thomas Tucker, *George Washington's Surprise Attack: A New Look at the Battle That Decided the Fate of America* (New York: Skyhorse Publishing, 2014), xvii.

[15]Richard M. Ketchum, *The Winter Soldiers* (Garden City, NY: Doubleday & Company, Inc., 1973), 325.

a number of men ever employed so short a space of time with greater and more lasting effects upon the history of the world."[16]

In the campaign marked by the victories at Trenton and Princeton, the Continental Army and the militia supporting its efforts defeated a better trained and more experienced enemy force in spite of the hardships encountered by the Americans: shortages of supplies; brutal weather; desertions; expiring enlistments; and the effects of malnutrition, disease, and exhaustion. In the fullness of time, their performance would be judged as "one of the most brilliant in military history."[17]

This sentiment was echoed by Thomas Paine, the English immigrant and now ardent American patriot. His pamphlet, *Common Sense*, had stirred Americans to support independence from Britain early in 1776, selling more than 100,000 copies within four months, and its sequel, *The American Crisis* - which legend has it was written on the head of a drum by Paine while volunteering with the army - stirred them to support resistance against Britain at the end of 1776. Not surprisingly, he exulted in the Americans' coup.

Paine would write in Number V of *The American Crisis* in March 1778:

> *The conquest of the Hessians at Trenton by*
> *the remains of a retreating army is an instance*
> *of heroic perseverance very seldom to be met*

---

[16]McCullough, *1776*, 291

[17]Fischer, 367.

with. And the victory over the British troops at Princeton, by a harrassed and wearied party, who had been engaged the day before and marched all night without refreshment, is attended with such a scene of circumstances and superiority of Generalship, as will ever give it a place on the first line in the history of great actions.[18]

The fortunes of war are often impacted by contingency, and the American successes at this time owed no less to fortuitous circumstances. For example, it is worth remembering in this context how weather impacted the campaign. First, there was the winter storm that convinced the Hessians in Trenton that there was no need to fear an attack from across the river on Christmas night. Then there were the muddy roads that, together with stiff American resistance, slowed the advance of British and Hessian troops under Gen. Cornwallis from Princeton to Trenton during the unseasonably warm weather on 2 January 1777, leaving them without enough daylight to launch a full-scale attack against the Continental forces along the Assunpink Creek. Finally, there was the dramatic drop in temperatures during the night of 2 January that made the dirt roads solid enough for Washington to elude Cornwallis under the cover of darkness and transport his troops and artillery some 12 miles during a dramatic overnight march that culminated in the final American victory of the "Ten Crucial Days" at Princeton on 3 January. Describing the successful river crossing and the engagement at Trenton

---

[18]Thomas Paine, *Collected Writings* (New York: The Library of America, 1955), 157.

on 26 December to his wife, Lucy, three days after the event, Washington's chief of artillery, Col. Henry Knox (about to be promoted to brigadier general for his efforts) wrote: "Providence seemed to have smiled upon every part of this enterprise."[19]

The narrative that follows does not discount the effects of providence, weather, sound strategy, and able leadership in bringing about the results achieved by American arms during the "Ten Crucial Days." It does, however, seek to recognize the importance of the contributions that were made by lesser known individuals in the course of this campaign, and is grounded in a belief that a closer look at the exploits of obscure but heroic figures such as these may yield a deeper understanding of the dynamics behind great events and their historical context.

The ten Americans whose stories are the subject of this account were a mixed lot in terms of their backgrounds and their experiences during the struggle for independence:

> They included five colonels (one of whom served as commissary general of the Continental Army and two of whom were later promoted to general), two captains, a sergeant, and two civilians caught up in the conflict.

> Only three are known to have served in the military before 1775. (In the early days

---

[19]William S. Stryker, *The Battles of Trenton and Princeton* (Boston: Houghton, Mifflin and Company, 1898), 372.

of the Revolution, it was quite common for men to be commissioned as officers in the Continental Army and the militia based on their social standing in the community rather than demonstrated military skill or experience.)

Before the revolution, they were variously engaged in commerce, farming, government, the law, medicine, the ministry, sailmaking, and shipping.

The age at enlistment of the nine who signed up for military service in 1775 and 1776 ranged from about 20 to 62 years old.

They came from seven of the 13 colonies that established the new American nation: Connecticut, Delaware, Massachusetts, New Jersey, New York, Pennsylvania, and Virginia.

Two were Irish immigrants, and one was a woman whose identity is still unknown to us.

They contributed to the war effort in various ways during the period covered by this narrative: conveying troops by boat; feeding and otherwise supplying the soldiers of the Continental Army; caring for the wounded; diverting enemy forces away from the main focus of military activity at a critical moment; engaging in direct combat; organizing, drilling, and leading infantry; and commanding artillery.

One died in battle, and two others did not live to see the end of the conflict.

These individuals, with the possible exception of the mysterious widow whose exploits may have been inadvertent, became committed adherents to a cause for which they were willing to pledge their lives, their fortunes, and their sacred honor, much as our founding fathers had already proclaimed in the Declaration of Independence. They collectively made a vital contribution to winning the great struggle in which they played a part because they made a crucial difference in the outcome of the Revolution's most crucial days. When a new nation needed heroes such as these in order to survive during its darkest hour, they came to its rescue.

In the end, the exploits of these resilient patriots yield tales of courage, competence, and cunning that tell us something about who we were, who we are, and who we might be as a people and a country. Perhaps stories such as these can serve as a source of renewed pride in the common heritage and purpose of those who are privileged to live in what may be the oldest democracy in the modern world - and a source of inspiration to the many who yearn for a greater public consciousness of what unites Americans rather than what divides them.

Such an appeal to the common interest was conveyed to our citizenry in the earliest days of the republic as follows: "The name of AMERICAN, which belongs to you, in your national capacity, must always exalt the just pride of patriotism, more than any appellation derived from local discriminations."[20] In so doing, the nation's first chief executive exhorted his fellow countrymen to assume a greater sense of national identity as he approached the end of his presidency in 1796 and prepared to retire from public life. It was a point well taken in George Washington's farewell address to the American people.

---

[20]Ron Chernow, *Washington: A Life* (New York: The Penguin Press, 2010), 755.

A replica Durham boat at Washington Crossing Historic Park (Washington Crossing, Pennsylvania)

Chapter 2

William Blackler

> *. . . in every human Breast, God has implanted a Principle, which we call love of Freedom; it is impatient of Oppression, and pants for Deliverance.*
>
> - Phillis Wheatley, African American Poet, from a letter to the Reverend Samson Occom, 11 February 1774, published in two Boston newspapers

According to tradition, Capt. William Blackler commanded the boat that took George Washington across the Delaware River on 25 December 1776.[1] The Continental Army stormed back into New Jersey that

---

[1]Fischer, 219.

night across an ice-choked waterway by Durham boat and ferry and undertook a nearly ten-mile, snow-filled march to Trenton to surprise the Hessian brigade occupying the town. In many cases, the soldiers who made this march wore shoes that were falling apart or tied rags around their feet because they had no shoes, leaving a bloodstained trail in the snow to mark the army's movements.

Accounts of the crossing from that period attest to Capt. Blackler having "had command of the boat in which Gen. Washington was rowed across."[2] He served in the 14th Massachusetts Continental Regiment from Marblehead under Col. John Glover, known as the Marblehead Regiment or more informally the Marbleheaders, and (according to at least one study of the crossing) was viewed as one of Glover's most trusted officers.[3] While it is unlikely that Glover would have assigned the responsibility of carrying his commander-in-chief safely across the river to anyone whom he did not hold in the highest regard, his choice paid homage to the individual tasked with managing perhaps the most important boat ride in American history.

At age 36, Blackler had been a successful merchant and shipper and would provide valued service to the patriot cause beyond the vital role that he played in the Delaware River crossing. This Marblehead native raised a militia company in his hometown as early as 1773, training and equipping its men at his own expense. He joined what

---

[2] Frank A. Gardner, "Glover's Marblehead Regiment in the War of the Revolution," *Massachusetts Magazine* (I:2, April 1908), www.archive.org.

[3] Tucker, 26.

became the Continental Army in April 1775 and was appointed a captain in June. In addition, he outfitted a privateering vessel that sported a dozen cannon and made its initial voyage to raid British shipping in September 1776. After the "Ten Crucial Days" ended, Blackler went on to see further action in the war before being severely wounded at the Battle of Bemis Heights, also known as the Second Battle of Saratoga, in October 1777.

The Marblehead Regiment was considered to be one of the best in the army.[4] Its composition was distinctive as a military unit because its ranks were filled by recruits from fishing towns on the north shore of Massachusetts such as Beverly, Lynn, Marblehead, and Salem, and many of these soldiers had made their living at sea.

What was also distinctive about the regiment's composition was its ethnic diversity; Col. Glover welcomed his fellow shipmates from these seaport towns into his ranks, including Indian and African American soldiers. This posed an issue for some in the army, including the commander-in-chief, who overcame his reservations and learned to accommodate himself to these circumstances. Although the African American sailors and fishermen serving in the Marblehead Regiment were free men, it is worth noting that at the outset of the Revolution, slaves brought from Africa and the West Indies to the colonies accounted for the largest non-English component of the total population in America (perhaps as many as half a million people or about 20 percent).

---

[4]Fischer, 21.

The paradox of American colonists fighting for their freedom from British imperial rule while enslaving a sizable portion of the new nation's inhabitants was not lost on our founding fathers. As Gordon Wood reminds us, "All the revolutionary leaders became aware of the excruciating contradiction between their revolution on behalf of liberty and American slavery."[5] But this awareness did not lessen "the cruel irony of slavery being preserved despite the brave service of many black Americans" in the war.[6]

African American soldiers fought at Trenton, including non-Marbleheaders such as Pvt. Jacob Francis, a 22-year-old former indentured servant born in Amwell, New Jersey, who served in the 16th Regiment of Massachusetts Continentals under Col. Paul Dudley Sargent.[7] By the end of the war, they had accounted for five percent of all those who served in the Continental Army, representing some 5,000 soldiers.[8] Ultimately, according to Henry Wiencek, "The commander needed his black troops because white enlistment was precarious."[9] In the process, Washington's

---

[5]Gordon S. Wood, *Revolutionary Characters: What Made the Founders Different* (New York: The Penguin Press, 2006), 38.

[6]Henry Wiencek, *An Imperfect God: George Washington, His Slaves, and the Creation of America* (New York: Farrar, Straus and Giroux, 2003), 218.

[7]William M. Dwyer, *The Day Is Ours!: November 1776 - January 1777: An Inside View of the Battles of Trenton and Princeton* (New York: The Viking Press, 1983), 257. See also Karina Robinson, Francis, Jacob (1754-1836). www.blackpast.org., and *Jacob Francis, 1754–1836, African American. Crossroads of the American Revolution National Heritage Area.* www.revolutionarynj.org.

[8]John Ferling, *Almost a Miracle: The American Victory in the War of Independence* (New York: Oxford University Press, 2007), 344.

[9]Wiencek, 215.

army, led by a slaveholder, "became the first integrated national institution in the United States."[10] Perhaps not so coincidentally, its commander-in-chief later became the only founding father to free those he held in servitude (albeit posthumously by a provision in his will that took effect upon the death of his wife, Martha).

By their actions as well as their composition, the Marbleheaders had already assumed a distinctive role in the army. Back in August, they had proven their value to the cause when they rescued more than 9,000 of Washington's beaten troops from Brooklyn after the disaster at the Battle of Long Island by rowing them across the East River to Manhattan under the cover of nighttime darkness and early morning fog. By doing so, they eluded an enemy who would otherwise have captured a significant portion of the total American force in New York. Now their mission was to transport the Continentals across another river in the dark, this time moving toward the enemy. They would be joined by other mariners and seafaring types from the Philadelphia waterfront and locals from Pennsylvania and New Jersey who knew how to navigate the river at night.

On Washington's orders, the Durham boats used in the Delaware crossing were rounded up along the Delaware and Lehigh rivers; this effort was directed by three captains in the Hunterdon County militia: Daniel Bray, Jacob Gearhart, and Thomas Jones. According to tradition, the boats were concealed behind Malta Island below New Hope on the Pennsylvania side and several miles north of

---

[10]Fischer, 2.

McConkey's Ferry, where the crossing occurred.[11] (Malta Island is no longer discernible due to topographical changes since that time.) Other types of boats, including virtually anything that floated, were also gathered as part of this effort and moored in creeks and behind wooded islands on the Pennsylvania side so as to deprive the enemy of their use.

The Durham boats were so named because they were designed by engineer Robert Durham and built by the Durham Ironworks or Durham Furnace near Easton, Pennsylvania. These craft, which generally ranged from 30 to 60 feet in length, are estimated to have each carried between 30 and 40 soldiers, in addition to a crew of several rowers and a captain who acted as a pilot and steered the boat by means of a long "sweep" oar protruding from its stern. There were no seats on these boats, as they were not designed to carry passengers, but rather were used to transport cargo such as coal, flour, furs, grain, iron ore, pig iron, timber, and whiskey. So the Continental soldiers would have been required to stand during the crossing.

An ongoing debate persists among students of the crossing about whether Washington took a Durham boat or a ferry across the Delaware or, to put it another way, which type of boat Captain Blacker would have piloted across the river that night with his commander-in-chief in tow. The weight of recent scholarship suggests that it was a Durham boat. Robert Middlekauff's history of the

---

[11]Peter Osborne, *No Spot In This Far Land Is More Immortalized: A History of Pennsylvania's Washington Crossing Historic Park* (Yardley, PA: Yardley Press, 2014), 53.

Revolution tells us that Washington "crossed with the advance party in Durham boats."[12] Other historians such as David Hackett Fischer and Phillip Thomas Tucker appear to concur.[13] William Dwyer's narrative also falls into line on this point.[14] In addition, Fischer and Tucker report that Pvt. John Russell of Marblehead served as an oarsman on Blackler's boat.[15]

Washington knew that the crossing would, in biographer Ron Chernow's phrase, "produce either storied success or utter calamity, and he seemed ready to pay the price."[16] As he crossed the river in advance of the main part of his army, the determined commander confronted such daunting issues as the ice that was pushed along by a swift current and the uncertain prospect of getting the entire army across in one night when it had taken several days for it to cross in the opposite direction during the first week of December.

---

[12]Middlekauff, 366.

[13]Fischer implies that Washington crossed in a Durham boat because in all likelihood Capt. Blackler would have commanded a Durham boat during the crossing rather than a ferry boat, which would probably have been operated by ferrymen who worked at the McConkey's Ferry or the Johnson's Ferry at that time. Tucker explicitly states that Washington crossed in a Durham boat per the note below ("With a white piece of paper pinned to his hat") that cites to page 26 of his book. Also, see the note immediately following to page 233 of William Dwyer's book where he states that the "Marbleheaders relied heavily on Durham boats." Although Dwyer does not specifically reference Blackler, the obvious inference to be drawn from this is that if Washington was in the boat commanded by the Marbleheader captain, it would probably have been a Durham boat.

[14]Dwyer, 233.

[15]Fischer, 219, and Tucker, 26.

[16]Chernow, *Washington*, 272.

The challenge of transporting seven brigades of infantry in the Durham boats, including 2,400 soldiers who each carried 60 rounds of ammunition and a three-day supply of rations, was formidable enough. But the army also had to carry across on flat-bottomed ferry boats - procured from the McConkey's Ferry on the Pennsylvania side and the Johnson's Ferry on the New Jersey side - some 50 to 100 horses, 18 artillery pieces, and an unknown number of ammunition wagons. And then there was the weather, "a bone-chilling mixture of rain, sleet, and wind that soaked everything"; by 11:00 p.m., it had degenerated into "a grim northeaster" that "began to churn up the waters" as "snow and hail pelted men exposed in the boats."[17]

These harsh conditions turned Washington's battle plan into the first casualty of the battle. Two other American units were supposed to cross over from the Pennsylvania side and support the attack on Trenton, including some 800 Pennsylvania militia under Gen. James Ewing stationed opposite the southern end of Trenton and another 1,800 militia from Pennsylvania and New England under Col. John Cadwalader in Bristol. But the buildup of ice on the river prevented these forces from getting across that night, leaving Washington's two divisions to carry out the attack on their own. In addition, the weather conditions and the challenge involved in moving artillery across the river extended the time required for the crossing. The whole army did not reach the New Jersey side until about 3:00 a.m. and did not start marching to Trenton until

---

[17]Stryker, 133.

about 4:00 a.m. They were several hours behind schedule because Washington and his generals had planned to get everyone and everything across by midnight in order to arrive in Trenton while it was still dark. Instead, they would not reach their objective until after daybreak, which occurred at about 7:20 a.m.

The captain and crew on each of the boats that carried Washington and his soldiers across the river on Christmas night had to contend with a variety of weather-related challenges: the lack of visibility due to cloud cover that obscured a full moon; an additional 50 to 80 feet that each boat had to be rowed across a river swollen by continuous precipitation; a swift current pushing the boats off course; sheets of ice shoving the boats, which must have been especially unnerving to the passengers who in most cases did not know how to swim at a time when the vast majority of people lacked that skill (including sailors); and a bitterly cold wind blowing in the faces of the captain and crew.

According to William Stryker's account, "The jagged ice floated swiftly by and struck the boats so severely that they could be handled only with the greatest difficulty."[18] This same narrative noted that had the Marbleheaders not "lent a willing and skillful hand," the crossing "would no doubt have failed" for they "were then . . . as they had been in New York harbor . . . when the retreat was made from Long Island, the men on whom all relied to see the army safely landed."[19]

---

[18]Ibid., 133.

[19]Ibid., 133-134.

As much as the weather plagued the Continental Army that night, it proved to be a double-edged sword. Its severity lulled the Hessians in Trenton into a false sense of security to the extent that they did not send patrols up the river as was their custom during less harsh climatic conditions, and the blizzard that reached full force after the Americans had crossed the river screened their movement south. When they arrived in Trenton at about 8:00 a.m., they found the enemy unprepared for the Continentals' assault.

It should be noted that European armies of the time, such as the Hessians, generally did not campaign during the winter months nor in inclement weather or at night. The American intruders might be said to have broken all these rules on 26 December, and in that sense, Washington's victory at Trenton could be construed as the product of a uniquely American style of waging war in the 18th century. On a more personal level, "Washington had been indelibly imprinted by his time in the wilderness [as a young soldier], and it would be the hit-and-run style of the native way of war that remained his forte" throughout the Revolution.[20]

Although a significant number of Continental soldiers who participated in the crossing would succumb to disease, exposure, exhaustion, or malnutrition in the days and weeks following the event, the bottom line for the army on that fateful night was that it made its legendary crossing without losing a single soldier, cannon, horse,

---

[20]Philbrick, 68.

wagon, or boat. Col. Glover's Marbleheaders and other crew members rowing the Durham boats were most responsible for that, and one of the crew members later asserted - perhaps in something of an overstatement, but with some justification - that the victory over the Hessians "was won by Glover and Durham."[21] In any event, Capt. Blackler was the man most responsible for the commander-in-chief arriving safely on the New Jersey side of the river to pursue his rendezvous with glory on a snowy Trenton battlefield.

Blackler resigned his army commission after being wounded during the Saratoga campaign the following year and returned to Marblehead, where he would continue his life as a sea captain and merchant. He died in 1818 at age 78.

The image we are best left with of his service to the patriot cause is evoked by the following passage from a recent account: "With a white piece of paper pinned to his hat, like other Continental officers as Washington had specified to designate rank that could be seen in the darkness, Blackler commanded the sturdy Durham boat that carried Washington into the very vortex of the Delaware's swirling, dark waters."[22] In short, William Blackler was the man who uniquely assisted the Continental Army's Christmas night 1776 enterprise. At the place known today as Washington Crossing, he crossed Washington.

---

[21]Dale, 39.

[22]Tucker, 26.

Joseph Trumbull (NYPL Digital Collection)

Chapter 3

Joseph Trumbull

> *In such a Cause every Post is honourable in which a Man can serve his Country.*
>
> - Gen. George Washington, Commander-in-Chief of the Continental Army, from a letter to Col. Benedict Arnold, 14 September 1775

Napoleon Bonaparte once opined that, "An army marches on its stomach."[1] If his observation was correct, nobody did more to keep the soldiers of the Continental Army on the move during the dark days of 1776 than the man who fed them, Joseph Trumbull.

---

[1]Dr. Cliff Welborn, "Supply Line Warfare," *Army Logistician* (40:6, November-December 2008), www.almc.army.mil.

The Trumbull family hailed from Connecticut and played an important role during the Revolution, led by Jonathan, the father who served as Governor from 1776 to 1784 and was an ardent supporter of the patriot cause. His youngest and most famous son, the artist John, served under Washington and earned renown through his paintbrush by employing heroic imagery to capture dramatic moments in the struggle for independence. Another son, Jonathan Jr., ably performed the duties of paymaster for Washington's army. It has been said that "what Lee implied in Virginia, or Adams in Massachusetts, or Livingston in New York and New Jersey, Trumbull signified in Connecticut."[2]

It was, however, the oldest son who arguably performed the greatest service to the cause of the young nation, particularly when the "glorious cause" teetered on the edge of total failure in late 1776. That was Joseph, who served as the first commissary general of the Continental Army, from 19 July 1775 to 2 August 1777, with the rank of colonel. He secured that congressional appointment through George Washington's influence after coming to Washington's attention as commissary general for Connecticut's military forces in early 1775. Trumbull was born in Lebanon, Connecticut, and like his father graduated from Harvard and became a successful merchant. He then served in the Connecticut General Assembly and was elected to the First Continental Congress in 1774 as an

---

[2]Fischer, 158.

alternate delegate. His record and service spoke of him as "an honest man."[3]

Trumbull was 38 years of age when appointed to the post of Commissary General of Stores and Provisions, and by all accounts served admirably in that position. He was "remarkably successful" in creating a system by which the states would supply the Continental Army and was highly regarded by his military peers; indeed, his commander-in-chief observed: "Few armies if any have been better and more plentifully supplied than the troops under Mr. Trumbull's care."[4]

The Continental Army patterned its supply system after that of the British Army, with a commissary department that was responsible for overseeing the provision of food and general supplies to the troops. By 1776, this department had become "the largest economic organization in the colonies."[5]

Trumbull's effort to feed Washington's troops in late 1776 "was a saga in its own right." The army was unable to obtain supplies from New Jersey after retreating across the Delaware River in early December, and it could not forage from its new base of operations in Bucks County, Pennsylvania. The army's commissary officers reported that local farmers would not sell nor millers grind if they were to be paid in Continental dollars, and Trumbull "was

---

[3]Ibid., 158

[4]Ibid., 158.

[5]Ibid., 268.

able to feed the army only by a continental effort, which operated at the limits of possibility in early America." [6]

The staples of the soldier's diet at this point were largely hard bread or biscuit and heavily salted meat. The means of supplying these comestibles were so limited in the middle states that the commissary general was forced to bring them in from a considerable distance: "flour from the great Virginia grain plantations along the James, Rappahannock, and Potomac Rivers" and salt meat "by wagon from New England, over a long and dangerous route through the New York Highlands." Trumbull moved to New England in the fall of 1776, over Washington's objections, as that region remained his "strongest source of supply for provisions, clothing, and money."[7]

Richard Ketchum writes of Trumbull's efforts at this time: "the indefatigable commissary general . . . was making some progress by darting here and there, gathering up whatever he could lay hands upon, but . . . was continually hampered by a shortage of funds for these purposes."[8] In addition, the states "appointed numerous commissaries, creating senseless competition."[9]

The task of feeding Washington's army posed an ongoing challenge throughout the war. It has been observed that Trumbull and deputy commissary general

---

[6]Ibid., 268.

[7]Ibid., 268.

[8]Ketchum, 266.

[9]John Mack Faragher, *The Encyclopedia of Colonial and Revolutionary America* (New York: Da Capo Press, 1996), 427.

Walter Livingston were "either incredibly capable or extremely fortunate, for great crises never occurred on their watch."[10]   According to one scholar, Trumbull "performed as well as circumstances permitted," and those circumstances included "a group of deputy commissioners discontented almost from the beginning of their service at Congress' refusal to allow them compensation on the basis of their purchases."[11]

Unfortunately, Trumbull's successors would be less successful in their efforts than he was. The specter of bribery reared its ugly head as the Continentals' supply system became "shamefully tainted with corruption and profiteering from one end to the other, and Congress was unable, or unwilling, to do much about it."[12] As the conflict progressed, the difficulties encountered in keeping the army adequately supplied became a greater impediment to its ability to prosecute the war.

Trumbull resigned as commissary general when the Continental Congress reorganized that office into two branches, one for purchases and the other for issues, but he served as commissioner of the newly created Board of War until his resignation in April 1778 due to ill health. He returned to Lebanon, Connecticut, where he died three months later at age 41.

---

[10]Ferling, *Almost a Miracle*, p. 278.

[11]Robert Middlekauff, *Washington's Revolution: The Making of America's First Leader* (New York: Alfred A. Knopf, 2015), p. 169.

[12]Ferling, *Almost a Miracle*, p. 569.

The importance of the efforts made by the Continental Army's first commissary general to feed young America's soldiers and the competence that he demonstrated in meeting the challenges of his position were such that "Joseph Trumbull's quiet labors behind the scenes allowed Washington to keep an army in being. He made his greatest contribution during the black times of 1776."[13] The Continentals were desperately short of various supplies by the time they crossed the river on Christmas night, but food was not one of those missing items. At this pivotal moment in the Revolution, Joseph Trumbull had quite literally sustained these troops - and perhaps the patriot cause - for each soldier who traversed the ice-laden waterway was provided with a three-day supply of rations before embarking on the most important offensive that Washington's army would ever undertake.

---

[13]Fischer, p.158.

Samuel Griffin (Gilbert Stuart)

Chapter 4

Samuel Griffin & the Mysterious Widow

Perhaps there are no people on earth, in whom a spirit of enthusiastic zeal is so readily enkindled, and burns so remarkably conspicuous, as among the Americans. . . . The energetic operation of this sanguine temper, was never more remarkably exhibited, than in the change instantaneously wrought in the minds of men, by the capture of Trenton at so unexpected a moment.

- Mercy Otis Warren, from her *History of the Rise, Progress and Termination of the American Revolution,* 1805

The "odd couple" of a Continental Army colonel and an anonymous widow in Mount Holly, New Jersey helped to ensure the triumph of Washington's army at the First Battle of Trenton by diverting Hessian troops who might otherwise have come to the aid of Col. Rall's beleaguered soldiers when the American brigades arrived at their doorstep on the morning of 26 December 1776.

Samuel Griffin was a 30-year-old lawyer from Virginia - a native of Richmond County - who had been wounded in the heel at the Battle of Harlem Heights, a relatively minor engagement fought during the New York campaign some three months before (near the present site of Columbia University). Col. Griffin found himself in southern New Jersey in early December "with a small force of Virginia artillery and a few Continental infantry from Pennsylvania" after Washington's main force had withdrawn across the Delaware River to Pennsylvania.[1] During the second week in December, Gen. Israel Putnam, the American military officer in command at Philadelphia, dispatched militia across the river at Washington's direction in order to launch an attack against the Hessian forces in the Mount Holly area as a diversionary tactic. At the same time, additional militia rallied to Griffin in response to widespread reports of depredations committed by enemy soldiers against the civilian population in New Jersey. By mid-December, Griffin had at least 500 troops at his command, largely militia from Cumberland, Gloucester, and Salem counties. Their numbers continued to grow, and on 14 December they began an advance from Haddonfield, about 30 miles below Trenton, to Mount Holly.

Col. Carl von Donop had overall command of the Hessian forces in the Trenton-Bordentown-Burlington

---

[1]Fischer, 198.

area and was posted at Bordentown, about six miles south of Trenton. He served as the superior officer to Col. Rall, who commanded the garrison at Trenton. Donop was alerted to the movement of Griffin's militia on 22 December by a Tory agent named Barzella Haines, who observed them at Mount Holly the day before, and by Col. Thomas Stirling, who commanded the 42nd Highland Regiment at Black Horse, about six miles south of Burlington. Haines reported that "they were not above eight hundred, near one half boys, and all of them militia a very few from Pennsylvania excepted."[2] Stirling advised Donop that "if it is necessary to keep this Country for the Winter, . . . we should not wait to be attacked. . . . You sir, with the troops at Bordentown, should come here and attack. I am confident we are a match for them."[3]

In response to this intelligence, Col. von Donop determined to counter Griffin's move. The Americans had attacked the British and Hessian outposts at the Petticoat Bridge at Blackhorse on the 22nd; however, the next day, Donop launched a counterattack that forced Griffin and his outnumbered militia to fall back. According to the Hessian colonel, "In order to get rid of these troublesome guests I marched early . . . in the morning toward Mount Holly with the 42nd [Scottish] Regiment and the [Hessian] Block and Linsing Battalions. I met several hundred rebels in front near the Meeting House [in Mount Holly]. They took to flight after firing a few shots and retired with the others

---

[2]Ibid., 198.

[3]Ibid., 199.

toward Moorestown. Their strength was about 1,000 men and they were commanded by Colonel Griffin."[4]

Even though Griffin's militia "did little more than fire a few rounds and retreat in the skirmishes of December 22 and 23, they accomplished something that turned out to be of great tactical importance" by drawing Donop's forces from the Bordentown area down to Mount Holly.[5] The value of this diversion was recognized by Col. Joseph Reed of Washington's staff, who wrote: "Colonel Griffin retired skirmishing with the enemy a few miles with little loss on either side & bringing off his artillery with him. This manouver . . . had a happy effect as it drew off Count Donop who then commanded at Bordentown, with his whole force to Mount Holly."[6]

An American loyalist, Joseph Galloway of Philadelphia, concurred with Reed's assessment of the importance of the Hessian troop movement. He also noted that Donop had compounded its effect by not withdrawing to his post after driving off Griffin's militia, for "instead of immediately returning to Bordentown to support Colonel Rall, he remained loitering . . . without having a single enemy to oppose."[7]

Col. von Donop elected to remain in Mount Holly on the night of 23 December and was there the next day (as explained in the journal of the Hessian Linsing battalion)

---

[4]Dwyer, 214

[5]Ibid. 215.

[6]Ibid., 216.

[7]Ibid., 217.

in order, "first, to let the people longing for protection take an oath of allegiance to the King and, second, to collect forage and food in the neighborhood."[8] He was still there on Christmas day with his troops, more than a full day's march from Col. Rall's brigade in Trenton, even though this was clearly at variance with what was intended by the British command. Gen. Howe had purposely stationed British and Hessian forces in the various outputs extending across northern and central New Jersey so that they would be within close enough distance of each other to provide mutual support in the event of an attack.

While at Mount Holly, Donop took up quarters in the house of a woman who was described by one of his officers, Capt. Johann Ewald, as an "exceedingly beautiful young widow of a doctor." According to a local resident, Margaret Morris, "all the women removed from the Town except one widow of our acquaintance" prior to the Hessians' arrival, and Donop, whom Capt. Ewald observed to be "exceedingly devoted to the fair sex," was apparently smitten with her.[9]

Ewald attributed momentous consequences to this dalliance between the colonel and the young woman. As he later lamented,

> *This great misfortune, which surely caused the utter loss of the thirteen splendid provinces of the Crown of England, was due partly . . . to the fault of Colonel Donop, who was led by the nose to*

---

[8]Ibid., 217.

[9]Fischer, 199.

> *Mount Holly by Colonel Griffin, and detained there by love. . . . Thus the fate of entire Kingdoms often depends upon a few blockheads and irresolute men.* [10]

It has been speculated that the object of Col. von Donop's affections was none other than the seamstress Betsy Ross, thought by some to have sewed the first "Stars and Stripes" flag, the design of which was adopted by the Continental Congress as the flag of the United States in June 1777. There are a number of aspects to her life at that time that lend credence to this romantic hypothesis: youth; beauty; widowhood; support of the patriot cause; residence in Philadelphia and family connections in Gloucester County, New Jersey, where she visited from time to time; an acquaintance with Margaret Morris and George Washington; and the possible relationship of her late husband, John Ross, to a physician then practicing in Mount Holly named Alexander Ross.[11]

Still, there is no definitive evidence at this point to confirm the identity of this mysterious widow or to ascertain whether her presence in Mount Holly at the moment of Donop's arrival was intentional or coincidental. We cannot help but wonder, along with William Dwyer: "Had this young woman been purposely placed in Mount Holly to attract the attention of Donop, who was known to

---

[10]Ibid., 200.

[11]Ibid., 200.

be a ladies' man? Was she there as a spy? Both perhaps?"[12] In the end, all we are left with is conjecture.

What is not conjectural, however, is the significance of this episode in the context of the "Ten Crucial Days." Despite the failure of Col. Griffin's raid to do any serious damage to the enemy, it must be viewed as an important adjunct to the successful American assault on the Hessians at Trenton to the extent that it lured Col. von Donop and his troops in Bordentown away from their post. This meant that "Donop's attention was drawn away from the main focus of Washington's attack. Rather than being six miles from Trenton and able to react to an attack on Rall, Donop and his men were a distant 18 miles away on the morning of December 26."[13]

In a sense, what Griffin began, the mysterious widow finished. His militia drew Donop's soldiers away from the vicinity of Trenton, and she made certain - apparently with the Hessian colonel's eager assent - that he and his troops stayed away long enough to be a non-factor in the battle that gave Washington's army its first significant victory of the war. As noted by Dwyer, "whoever and whatever she was, the widow made a major contribution, perhaps unintentionally, to the American cause."[14]

Samuel Griffin went on to a successful political career in his home state, where he continued his public service

---

[12]Dwyer, 217.

[13]David Bonk, *Trenton and Princeton 1776-77: Washington crosses the Delaware* (New York: Osprey Publishing, 2009), 46.

[14]Dwyer, 217.

in various capacities: as a member of the Virginia Board of War, mayor of Williamsburg, a county sheriff, and a member of the state House of Delegates and then the U.S. House of Representatives. Upon his death in 1810 at age 64, the *Virginia Patriot* in Richmond paid tribute to him as "an old and meritorious Revolutionary Officer."[15]

Since we do not know the identity of the woman who charmed Col. von Donop into irrelevance when it came to having any role in the Trenton battle, there is nothing to tell of her subse-quent life story. We do know that her Hessian admirer received a mortal wound during an attack on Fort Mercer, on the Delaware River below Philadelphia, in October 1777, and died - reportedly in his own words - "a victim of my ambition and the avarice of my sovereign."[16]

The obscure but vital contribution made by the Mount Holly widow to the success of Washington's offensive in the waning hours of 1776 is a metaphor for the equally unheralded but important role played by American women during the Revolution. Only a few women would have been found in American military camps during the early years of the war as "camp followers" (a common practice for armies of the period); however, by 1777, their numbers had begun to increase rapidly and with that, their role as part of the army: "Women cooked for the army. They did the washing and cleaned the camps. They were ordered to work as nurses, and after combat they

---

[15]Col Samuel Griffin. www.findagrave.com.

[16]Stryker, 40n1.

gleaned the battlefield and stripped the dead of clothing and possessions."[17]

The role of women extended to combat, for as David Hackett Fischer notes,

> *No women are known to have crossed the Delaware River with Washington, but probably they were there. More than a few dressed as men and bore arms with the infantry. In the battle of Trenton, at least one woman who lived in the town took up arms and brought down a Hessian officer. One wonders if she might have had a personal score to settle with the men who occupied her village.*[18]

Later in the war, Deborah Sampson of Massachusetts fought with the Continental Army for more than two years while disguised as a soldier named Robert Shurtlieff. She saw action in the Yorktown campaign of 1781, and although her true gender was eventually detected by a physician who was treating her for an illness, the recognition of her meritorious service was reflected in the honorable discharge that she received in October 1783.[19]

The most legendary account of women in combat during the Revolution may be that of "Molly Pitcher" during the Battle of Monmouth in 1778, reputedly Mary Ludwig Hays of Carlisle, Pennsylvania. According to the

---

[17]Fischer, 384.

[18]Ibid., 384-385.

[19]Deborah Sampson (1760-1827), *National Women's History Museum*, www.nwhm.org/education-resources/biography/biographies/deborah-sampson.

tale, she "allegedly took up a rammer and helped fire the field gun previously operated by her mortally wounded husband, if the doubtful story is true."[20]

It is fact, and not legend, that women with the army - in addition to their roles cited above - made soap, herded sheep and cattle, milked cows, sometimes foraged for food, and even acted as "beasts of burden" carrying "bushel baskets on their backs." What is more, some "came under fire while lugging water to thirsty soldiers and to artillerymen who had to swab the barrels of their field pieces between rounds." Although only a small portion of American women ever entered a military camp during the war, many on the home front lent their support to the cause by making bullets, sewing, knitting, and spinning fabric for the soldiers. Some called themselves "daughters of liberty."[21] Perhaps, however, they would be better termed "mothers of a new nation."

---

[20]Ferling, *Almost a Miracle*, 306

[21]Ferling, *Whirlwind: The American Revolution and the War That Won It* (New York: Bloomsbury Press, 2015), 251.

Dr. John Riker assisting Lt. James Monroe in the background
of *The Capture of the Hessians at Trenton* (John Trumbull)

Chapter 5

John Riker

Patriotism is as much a virtue as justice, and is as necessary for the support of societies as natural affection is for the support of families.
- Dr. Benjamin Rush, from a letter *To His Fellow Countrymen: On Patriotism*, 20 October 1773

Dr. John Riker joined the early morning march of the Continental troops to Trenton after they crossed the Delaware River on Christmas night 1776 in order to attack the Hessian brigade occupying the town. On that same day, he would render a service to the patriot cause with significant ramifications for his country's history that extended far beyond the confines of the Revolution.

Riker, then 38 years old and a descendant of Dutch immigrants who came to America in 1638, was born and raised in Newtown on Long Island (Queens County, New York). Educated at the College of New Jersey (Princeton University today), he started his practice of medicine in New Jersey and in 1768 became a member of the Medical Society of New Jersey - the oldest state medical society in America, established in 1766. It appears that Riker may have moved back to New York prior to the Revolution and then returned to New Jersey in 1776 in order to escape the invading British and Hessians following their successful New York campaign.

Lt. James Monroe - who in 1776 was an 18-year-old officer less than a year removed from the College of William and Mary in Virginia - later wrote that Riker encountered Monroe when the latter's 3rd Virginia Continental Regiment passed Riker's Hunterdon County home while preceding the main body of troops as the army's advance guard.[1] The young physician emerged from his residence to find out why his dogs were barking and initially reacted to the disturbance in a hostile manner. He thought the intruders were British troops and ordered them off his property, being "violent and determined in his manner, and very profane," to the point that Monroe advised Riker to return

---

[1]The area traversed by Washington's troops after they crossed the Delaware River was then part of Hunterdon County. It is today part of Mercer County, which was established by the New Jersey State Legislature in 1838 by combining parts of Burlington, Hunterdon, Middlesex, and Somerset counties. The new county was named for Gen. Hugh Mercer of the Continental Army, who died from wounds sustained at the Battle of Princeton on 3 January 1777.

to his house or be taken prisoner.[2] But once the public-spirited doctor realized that these men were American soldiers, he warmed to their presence. He returned to his house to bring them food and offered his services to the army in the hope that "I may be of help to some poor fellow."[3] Monroe accepted his offer, and Riker waited with the Virginians for the rest of the army to appear. When it did, at about dawn, he joined Monroe's regiment on its march south.

During the First Battle of Trenton later that morning, Monroe was carried from the field when a large caliber musket ball severed an artery in his left shoulder, and he was on the verge of bleeding to death. The scene is described thus in one account: "With the lead ball passing though Monroe's breast and shoulder, the gaping wound appeared mortal . . . [but at] a makeshift field hospital . . . one physician hurriedly tied the severed artery in Monroe's shoulder just in time."[4] (It is reported in some accounts that Monroe and other American soldiers were wounded by friendly fire from their side while fighting in the narrow streets of the town where most of the battle occurred.[5])

Capt. William Washington, a distant cousin of the Continental Army's commander-in-chief, and Lt. Monroe

---

[2]Fischer, 231.

[3]Ibid., 231.

[4]Tucker, 349.

[5]Randy Kraft, "Crossroads At The Crossing: Turnaround Begins In Small Steps At Historic Park," *The Morning Call* (25 December 1994). www.articles.mcall.com.

had led their Virginia infantry in a furious charge down King Street. This was one of two thoroughfares running through Trenton, the other being Queen Street (known today as Warren and Broad Streets, respectively). The attackers seized two cannon that the Hessians were attempting to fire at the onrushing Virginians during a pivotal moment in the battle. In the process, Capt. Washington was struck by musket fire in both hands and then Monroe, who had relieved him, was hit as well. There were very few American casualties during the battle, although historical accounts vary on this point. According to David Hackett Fischer, "the evidence indicates that two privates were killed in action, at least four or five died of exposure or illness, and three officers and two privates were wounded." [6]

By contrast, Fischer cites the following American estimates of losses among the three Hessian regiments in Col. Rall's brigade (Rall, Lossberg, and Knyphausen) as follows: 22 killed, including Rall; 84 severely wounded; and 812 taken prisoner but not severely wounded.[7] The dimensions of the Trenton victory can be measured by more than the disparity in casualties between the two sides, however. The Continentals captured all six enemy cannon, six wagons, 40 horses, one thousand muskets and bayonets, and a substantial quantity of ammunition.[8]

---

[6]Fischer, 406.

[7]Ibid., 405.

[8]Ferling, *Almost a Miracle*, 178.

The effort that was made to attend to the wounded Lt. Monroe is represented in a 1786 painting, "The Capture of the Hessians at Trenton" by John Trumbull (brother of Joseph Trumbull), which depicts the aftermath of the legendary engagement. In this celebrated work, the young officer can be seen lying on the ground behind the outstretched hand of Col. Rall, the mortally wounded Hessian commander. Monroe later wrote that the physician ministering to him stopped the bleeding by sticking his index finger into the wound and applying pressure to the artery.

Lt. Monroe was recognized for his service at Trenton by being promoted to captain and, after recuperating from his wound, would see further service in the war. He went on to enjoy a distinguished political career, becoming a U.S. senator, governor of Virginia, ambassador to France, secretary of state and war, and finally the fifth president of the United States in 1817, but he carried the musket ball from the First Battle of Trenton inside him for the rest of his life. At one point, surgeons attempted to remove the bullet but could not find it.

The surgery that averted Monroe's death on that wintry December battlefield by the Delaware River was performed by Dr. Riker. In addition, he dressed Monroe's wound daily for a period of about ten days during the latter's stay at Mr. Coryell's home in present-day New Hope, before Monroe was moved to another residence in Bucks County for the remainder of his convalescence.

However, it appears that the patient never learned the first name of the surgeon who saved his life or helped to care for him during the early stages of his recovery.[9]

Riker, whose "familiarity with the topography of New Jersey, enabled him to render valuable service on several occasions, as a guide to the army," continued to serve with the Continentals after the victory at Trenton.[10] Assigned as a surgeon to a New Jersey Continental regiment, he was captured during an engagement with a loyalist regiment near New Brunswick in October 1779 but freed as part of a prisoner exchange shortly afterwards. When the war ended, he returned to his native Newtown and practiced medicine there until his death in 1794 at age 56.

John Riker's support of the Revolution fit into a broader context of physician involvement with the patriot cause. This type of civic engagement was exemplified by Dr. Joseph Warren, who played a leading, and even inspirational, role in the Massachusetts rebellion before his death at the Battle of Bunker Hill in 1775, and by Dr. Benjamin Rush, who signed the Declaration of Independence and served as a surgeon general in the Continental Army.

One observer explains this pattern of physician activism during the period of revolutionary turbulence as follows:

---

[9]Rick Britton, "James Monroe: Bona Fide Hero of the American Revolution," *Journal of the American Revolution Online Magazine* (31 January 2013), www.allthingsliberty.com.

[10]Stephen Wickes, *History of Medicine in New Jersey* (Newark, NJ: Martin R. Dennis & Co., 1879), 372.

"Doctors were a significant portion of the most educated population, and their profession frequently put them into contact with prominent political leaders as well as the ordinary men and women whose lives were altered by their decisions. Simultaneous political involvement and medical practice are a rare combination in our times, but for Dr. Riker and his contemporaries, these were the right prescription for a new country." [11]

---

[11]Julie Gianakon, "Doctor Riker's decisión," *Hektoen International* (Spring 2014), www.hektoeninternational.org.

Continental Artillery 1777 - 1783 (painting by Jean Leffel from an illustration by H.A. Ogden and Lt. Charles Lefferts)

Chapter 6

Joseph White

> *Great works are performed, not by strength, but by perseverance . . .*
>
> - Samuel Johnson, from his novel, *The History of Rasselas, Prince of Abissinia*, 1759, as spoken by the character, Imlac

Sgt. Joseph White of Massachusetts fought in all three of the Continental Army's engagements during the "Ten Crucial Days." While conveying a somewhat self-interested attitude at times during his military service, he also demonstrated a determination and perseverance on behalf of the patriot cause that were best reflected by a gritty effort to rescue a cannon with a broken axle after the

First Battle of Trenton, when it might otherwise have been lost to the enemy. By so doing, he earned the recognition of the army's artillery commander, Henry Knox.

White is thought to have been born in Boston around 1755. In May 1775, he enlisted in what was soon to be designated as the Continental Army, in the wake of what Ralph Waldo Emerson six decades later indelibly termed the "shot heard round the world" at Lexington and Concord.[1] White was living in his family's home in Charlestown when he became caught up in the passion aroused by those legendary April skirmishes and signed up for eight months of duty as a bombardier in an artillery regiment. He soon became the regiment's assistant adjutant, whose duties were primarily administrative, owing to his spelling ability (as he would later explain).

The youthful assistant adjutant had occasion to meet the commander-in-chief later that year when he was ordered by the colonel in command of the regiment to deliver an oral message to General Washington in person. As White later described the scene, Washington asked him what his duties were, and when he responded, Washington observed that White was "very young to do that." White agreed but noted that he was "growing older every day." He then noticed that Washington turned to his visiting wife, Martha, and that they both smiled.[2]

---

[1]"The Shot Heard Round the Word: The Battles of Lexington and Concord:"Concord Hymn" - Ralph Waldo Emerson, www.constitutionfacts.com.

[2]Dwyer, 4-5.

Joseph White was one of the men who "became the core of the New England army," soldiers whose egalitarian ethos appeared as "indiscipline and disorder" to Washington when he assumed command of the Continentals during their siege of Boston in July 1775. These New Englanders, who disliked what they considered to be his "hierarchical attitudes," comprised two-thirds of Washington's army as late as June 1776, but he and they "slowly found a way to work together." The General "learned to listen, to reason, and to work through councils of war in which a majority of officers were Yankees." His men "learned that an army was not a town meeting, that somebody had to give orders, and that orders had to be obeyed. The result was an untidy and unstable compromise, which allowed an army of cantankerous Yankees to operate under a gentleman of Virginia."[3]

White, now an orderly sergeant, would be in Washington's presence again on 16 November 1776 along the banks of the Hudson River, as he was briefly on the scene when the general witnessed one of the worst defeats suffered by the Continental army in the entire war, the fall of Fort Washington. The young New Englander joined the army as it retreated across New Jersey into Pennsylvania under late autumn skies, buffeted by the adverse fortunes of war and harsh weather. As White later described it, "The sufferings we endured is beyond description - no tent to cover us at night - exposed to cold and rains day and night

---

[3]Fischer, 19-21.

- no food of any kind but a little raw flour."[4] Assigned to the 2nd Company, Pennsylvania State Artillery under Capt. Thomas Forrest, White and his fellow "cannoneers" found shelter and food in a Bucks County tavern after crossing over to the west bank of the Delaware River, although they actually obtained the edibles by force when the tavern keeper refused to accept "rebel money, as he called it."[5]

During the First Battle of Trenton on 26 December, White found himself in the thick of the fight as Capt. Forrest's battery went into action on the high ground above the town and fired down on the Hessian gunners. The gun to which the young sergeant was assigned became the only American artillery piece to be damaged in the battle, but not by enemy fire. When it fired its third shot, the axle splintered, presumably from the cumulative stress that was due to multiple river crossings, the long march to Trenton, and the effects of repeated blasts from its barrel with their violent recoils. The half dozen or so gunners of White's artillery crew, including soldiers from New England and Pennsylvania, were now without a piece to fire at the height of the battle. At that moment, the American artillery commander, Col. Knox, rode up on horseback and ordered White's men to join the charge down King Street that the 3rd Virginia Continental Regiment, led by Capt. William Washington and Lt. James Monroe, was about to launch in order to capture two cannon that the Hessians were attempting to fire at the Americans.

---

[4]Dwyer, 41.

[5]Ibid., 115.

White and his crew rushed the enemy guns along with the Virginians. "I hallowed as loud as I could scream to the men," he later wrote, "to run for their lives right up to the [enemy] pieces." The sergeant "was the first of his party to reach" the enemy cannon, and by now all but one of the Hessian gunners had retreated or been shot. Holding his sword over the cannoneer's head, White shouted: "Run, you dog!" The Hessian fled, and as White described it, "We put in a canister of shot (they had put in the cartridge before they left it,) and fired." The capture of these cannon, according to Major James Wilkinson,

> could not have been too highly appreciated for if the enemy had got his artillery into operation in a narrow street, it might have checked our movement and given him time to reform and reflect; and if he had retired across the bridge in his rear and taken post, he would have placed a defile between us, which in our half naked, half frozen condition, he ought to have defended against our utmost efforts, and we in turn might have been compelled to retreat, which would have been fatal to us.[6]

White and his fellow artillerists put their captured field piece to use against the Hessians "thanks to spare artillery equipment brought along for this express purpose as directed by Knox."[7] In capturing the two enemy guns, they and the other soldiers involved had succeeded at what was

---

[6]Ibid., 256-257.

[7]Tucker, 352.

perhaps the most hazardous exploit on that battlefield, one in which the officers leading the charge were both badly wounded - and James Monroe almost fatally. Afterwards, White rewarded himself for his heroics by securing "an elegant sword" from a dead Hessian officer.[8]

The army's return across the river "proved more difficult for many men than the crossing the day before." For some, that effort was even more challenging. White and his battery crew struggled to bring back their artillery piece with the broken axle, and he refused to abandon it even when Col. Knox ordered them to leave it behind. As he explained, "This piece was called the best in the regiment. I was determined to get it off. I hired four of our men and one of them had been a mate of a vessel; he contrived it and off we moved." The army's rearguard passed White's crew as it wrestled with the gun; again Knox ordered them to leave it and again the sergeant refused, explaining that he would rather risk being captured by the enemy "than to leave now we had got so far." The army disappeared in front of them but White's crew continued with their exertion, even being passed at one point by a party of Quakers on horseback that White initially mistook for enemy cavalry.[9]

Eventually the bone-weary but determined gun crew made it across the river with their gun. When Col. Knox spied the piece and asked White about it, the latter identified the gun as the one "that he [Knox] ordered to be left." The commander of artillery replied: "You are

---

[8]Dwyer, 261.

[9]Fischer, 257-258.

a good fellow . . . . I will remember you." With that, the exhausted sergeant "lay down upon the snow and took a nap; the heat of my body melted the snow and I sunk down to the ground."[10]

White again saw action at the Second Battle of Trenton on 2 January when his battery was among those that helped to stop the attempted advance of British and Hessian troops across the stone bridge over the narrow Assunpink Creek on the south side of town. The enemy launched three probes across the creek, and Washington's soldiers resisted with all the determination and desperation of an outnumbered army that had its back to the Delaware River - with no boats available to escape if its soldiers were pushed back or outflanked by their adversary. At that moment, as White's fellow New Englander, Capt. Stephen Olney, later recorded, "our army was in the most desperate situation I had ever known it."[11] The enemy advance was repulsed each time, and Sergeant White wrote of their final attempt: "They came on a third time. We loaded with canister shot and let them come nearer. We fired all together again, and such destruction it made, you cannot conceive. The bridge looked red as blood, with their killed and wounded and red coats."[12]

The artillerymen were part of the long American line that marched overnight from Trenton to Princeton to win its final victory of the "Ten Crucial Days" on 3 January. That

---

[10]Ibid., 258.

[11]Ibid., 304.

[12]Ibid., 306-307.

day, White was given command of an artillery piece that Capt. Benjamin Frothingham told him was in response to an order from Henry Knox because "he remembers what you did at Trenton."[13]   Firing canister into the enemy, White's gun was positioned along with other artillery on the American left and extended the line of cannon beyond the small British force that they faced. He recalled that the canister "made a terrible squeaking noise."[14]   (Canister and grapeshot were exploding shells of different sizes, in the form of a tin can and canvas bag, respectively, which were packed with objects such as iron balls, nails, pieces of chain, or stones, and directed at dense concentrations of enemy infantry.)

After the engagement at Princeton and with his term of enlistment having expired, Sergeant White was eager to return to Massachusetts, but he agreed to stay with the army for another two months in response to Capt. Frothingham's plea. On 1 March 1777, White "left the army and in about two weeks marched home safe and sound."[15] He returned to Boston, where he went into the printing business after the war.

In 1819, White applied for a pension as a Revolutionary War veteran and listed personal property worth a total of $61.55 on the application. At about 63 years of age, he was described as "a decrepid soldier capable only of being

---

[13]Dwyer, 329.

[14]Fischer, 334.

[15]Dwyer, 373.

a messenger and running errands."[16] In his later years, he published an account of his service in the Revolution, entitled "An [sic] Narrative of Events, As They Occurred from Time To Time, in the Revolutionary War; with an Account of the Battles, of Trenton, Trenton-Bridge, and Princeton."[17] His death notice, which appeared in the [Boston] *Daily Evening Transcript* on 15 March 1836, stated: "Mr. Joseph White, 81, died in Charlestown. He was a revolutionary pensioner and formerly a printer in this City."[18]

One observer's reading of White's memoir suggests that the then-youthful Continental soldier exhibited "a pattern of being sick during major battles" and "comes across as an operator within the ranks, looking out for himself a lot of the time," but notes that he "seems to have performed heroically at Trenton, helping to capture a British cannon and preserving an American one from being left behind."[19] From the information provided in the various accounts that we have of the "Ten Crucial Days," it seems reasonable to conclude that Sergeant White - model soldier or not - performed heroically on 26 December 1776 in helping to win the First Battle of Trenton and in salvaging an artillery piece that had clear and demonstrable value to the American cause. That he left the army shortly afterwards

---

[16]Kate Van Winkle Keller,"Joseph White: A Biographical Note and Preliminary Checklist of his Publications, 1783-1833." *American Antiquarian Society* (2008), 454, www.americananitquarian.org.

[17]Ibid., 451.

[18]Ibid., 451.

[19]J.L.Bell, "Joseph White: good speller, sickly soldier." *Boston 1775* (18 July 2006), www.boston1775.blogspot.com.

may not particularly commend him as a stalwart of the Revolution, but it should not detract from the role that he played at a decisive moment in the conflict.

Joseph White was part of the majority of soldiers in Washington's army who chose not to reenlist when their terms of service ended in 1775 and 1776. At the same time, new recruits - induced by offers of cash and land bounties - were enlisting for longer periods of up to three years. Most of those who left "felt that they had done their duty." They believed that it "was someone else's turn to sacrifice" or "they had grown disenchanted with soldiering" and its many attendant difficulties, including "boredom and the loss of one's freedom, not to mention loneliness, discomfort, poor or inadequate food, occasional insults and humiliation, and abundant danger." As William Dwyer put it, Joseph White was "an ordinary young man destined to take part in some extraordinary military action."[20] He did his job as he saw fit, braved danger, survived battle, played a part in the larger enterprise, and then went home. To that extent, his experience typified that of many a soldier in the American struggle for independence.

---

[20]Dwyer, 3.

Edward Hand (NYPL Digital Collection)

Chapter 7

Edward Hand

> *These are the times that try men's souls: The summer soldier and the sunshine patriot will, in this crisis, shrink from the service of his country; but he that stands it NOW, deserves the love and thanks of man and woman.*
>
> - Thomas Paine, from *The American Crisis*, Number I, 19 December 1776

Col. Edward Hand and the outnumbered soldiers under his command bravely and skillfully resisted the advance of the British and Hessian troops marching from Princeton to Trenton on 2 January 1777, and their delaying action bought the Continental Army enough time to successfully defend its position on the banks of the Assunpink Creek at the Second Battle of Trenton later that day. The clash at the creek became the precursor to Washington's audacious overnight end run around the enemy's left flank, followed by the next day's triumph at Princeton in the capstone event of the "Ten Crucial Days."

According to one description, "Hand looked the part of a soldier . . . tall, lean, and leathery, a natural leader."[1] He was 32 years old in 1776 and a native of Ireland, where he had pursued medical studies at Trinity College, Dublin. Hand enlisted as a surgeon's mate in the 18th Royal Irish Regiment in 1767 and came to America that year. In 1774, he resigned his commission and settled in Lancaster, Pennsylvania. A strong supporter of the Revolution, he helped organize the Lancaster County Associators and was commissioned a lieutenant colonel in command of a rifle unit known as the 1st Pennsylvania Continental Regiment. He was promoted to colonel a few months later, and his regiment joined the newly established Continental Army - camped in Cambridge outside Boston shortly after the battle at Bunker Hill in 1775 - as the first detachment of soldiers to report from beyond the boundaries of New England.

The 1st Pennsylvania soldiers, according to one description, "were backwoodsmen - tall, lean men who wore hunting shirts, leather leggings, and Indian moccasins, and carried that deadly long rifle which proved to be a thing of terror to the British and Hessians."[2] The skilled marksmen of Hand's outfit would become known

---

[1]Fischer, 296.

[2]Ketchum, 341.

for employing their American-made long rifles with lethal effect against the enemy. These weapons added a new dimension to the firepower of Washington's army.

As described by John Ferling,

They were a backcountry tool, made mostly in Pennsylvania and used there and in the Chesapeake colonies by men who hunted for much of their fresh meat. Unlike muskets, which were a smooth bore weapon, the long barrel of a rifle was etched, or 'rifled,' [on the inside] with seven or eight grooves. Rifling made the weapon accurate at a range of about two hundred yards, perhaps even three hundred, several times the reliable reach of a musket.[3]

The British Army had never taken to the use of rifles because they took longer to load and fire and could not accommodate a bayonet. Under the methods of warfare used in most European armies at this time, regiments fired in blocks rather than aiming individually, and to many officers, rifles were an unnecessary and wasteful expense. Instead, the redcoats continued to rely on the Brown Bess musket that was also used by Continental soldiers who were not in rifle companies. Although a highly unreliable weapon that was ineffective at a range of more than 80 to 100 yards, the use of the Brown Bess allowed the British to employ their "favorite tactic" - the bayonet charge "guaranteed to have a fearsome effect on an enemy."[4]

---

[3]Ferling, *Almost a Miracle*, 89.

[4]Ketchum, 219-221.

The reliance of British infantry tactics on the use of the bayonet reflected the fact that "a well-disciplined soldier could outrun the range of a musket in the time it took an enemy to reload."[5]

By December 1776, Col. Hand and his regiment "had fought in nearly every important engagement" since joining Washington's army, having seen action at the Battle of Long Island in August and in the subsequent New York campaign and retreat across New Jersey.[6] As part of the brigade commanded by Brig. Gen. Matthias Alexis de Roche Fermoy, a French recruit to the patriot cause, Hand's soldiers and the German Continental Regiment commanded by Col. Nicholas Haussegger (the only American regiment named for the ethnic identity of its soldiers) were among the first to engage the Hessians at Trenton on 26 December. Driving toward the Princeton Road lying northeast of the town, also known as the King's Highway, they assisted in cutting off what proved to be a futile attempt by Col. Rall's troops to skirt the Americans' left flank and escape in the direction of Princeton. This maneuver by Fermoy's brigade would help to seal the fate of an enemy force that was soon to be enveloped by the onrushing Continentals.

The events that ensued during the week following the First Battle of Trenton set the stage for the exploits of Hand's riflemen on the road from Princeton to Trenton.

---

[5]Richard Brookhiser, *Founding Father: Rediscovering George Washington* (New York: The Free Press, 1996) 31.

[6]Ibid., 341.

After the victory on 26 December, Washington marched his army and his prisoners back to Pennsylvania, but on the 29th and 30th, his men crossed the river once more and slogged back to Trenton. Washington learned that the Hessian troops below Trenton under Col. von Donop had pulled back from their outposts at Bordentown and Burlington in response to the attack on the Rall brigade, and he sought to take advantage of this development.

Once in Trenton, Washington was able to consolidate the American forces in the area, which included his brigades and the militia units led by Gen. James Ewing and Col. John Cadwalader that had also crossed over from Pennsylvania. He now had approximately 6,000 soldiers under his command, and they dug in along a three-mile stretch on the southern bank of the Assunpink Creek in lower Trenton in preparation for an enemy attack that they anticipated in response to the events of the 26th. This was a strong defensive position because it was on high ground overlooking a creek with very steep sides and, aside from a stone bridge near where the creek emptied into the Delaware River, offered very few places where an opposing army could cross.

While his men made ready, Washington delivered an impassioned plea to his soldiers whose one-year enlistments were to expire on 31 December, asking them not to go home but to remain with the army for another six weeks. He persuaded a bare majority of them to do so, aided by a promise to pay each soldier ten dollars in hard coin in exchange for his continued service.

The attack that the Americans anticipated came on 2 January, when Gen. Cornwallis led some 8,000 British and Hessian troops down the Princeton Road in the direction of Trenton. An able field commander, "Cornwallis was smart, daring, and tough."[7] He had pursued Washington's soldiers across New Jersey during their retreat to the Delaware River in November and early December, but had been unable to prevent their escape to the Pennsylvania side. Now, in the wake of the upstart rebels' shocking win at Trenton, Cornwallis's orders from his superior officer, Gen. William Howe, were straightforward - find the American army and destroy it. In short, his job was to finish the job.

The progress of Cornwallis's men toward Trenton on 2 January was slowed by muddy road conditions caused by rain the night before and unseasonably warm weather that day, but another impediment would prove to be even more problematic for his soldiers - Col. Hand and his Pennsylvania backwoodsmen. The British and Hessian vanguard reached the village of Maidenhead at about 11:00 a.m. and halted to allow the main body to come up. To this point, they had only encountered occasional harassing fire from scattered pickets; however, two miles south of the village in the woods behind the Big Shabakunk Creek, several American regiments, including Hand's, lay in waiting. They totaled about a thousand men and were commanded by Gen. Fermoy. As the enemy approached,

---

[7]Don Glickstein, *After Yorktown: The Final Struggle for American Independence* (Yardley, PA: Westholme Publishing, LLC, 2015), 12.

Fermoy suddenly mounted his horse and galloped toward Trenton, abandoning his command and leaving Col. Hand as the senior officer. Fortunately for the patriot cause, Hand was ready to lead and his men were ready to follow. Those "tough and undisciplined backcountry riflemen were devoted to him" and never proved it more than on this day.[8]

The soldiers under Hand's command included his regiment, the German Continental Regiment, and the 5th Virginia Continental Regiment led by Col. Charles Scott, supported by two guns from Capt. Thomas Forrest's Pennsylvania battery. As the flank and advance guards of Cornwallis's column approached, the Continentals unleashed a deadly fire that drove the enemy vanguard back into their main body and produced great confusion among them. Cornwallis was forced to throw the main body of his column into the fight and deploy artillery against the Continental sharpshooters hidden in the woods. The time it took their adversary to organize this effort and press their attack was crucially valuable to the American cause, for the longer it took Cornwallis to get to Trenton, the less time he would have to launch an attack against Washington before darkness interrupted his offensive.

Hand's resilient soldiers fell back in the face of superior enemy numbers but stubbornly fought a delaying action for much of the afternoon. They "waylaid their foe with a lethal fire from concealed positions in the untidy dark brown forests" and waged a series of "time-

---

[8]Fischer, 296.

consuming firefights before melting away to take up new positions further down the road." [9] Under heavy pressure and outnumbered more than six to one, the American units held off the advancing column for two hours until almost 3:00 p.m., when they began a slow retreat through the woods toward Trenton "in good order with all their equipment."[10] They had been jousting with the British and Hessians, with varying degrees of intensity, for some five hours, and had held them as long as they could. When Hand's defenders were about half a mile from the town, Washington, accompanied by Gens. Nathanael Greene and Henry Knox, rode up to encourage them and stress the importance of delaying the enemy until nightfall because the commander-in-chief had a plan that depended on holding off Cornwallis as long as possible.

By 4:00 p.m., with the shadows lengthening and the enemy force entering Trenton, Hand's men were falling back through the town. They directed a steady fire at their pursuers from behind the wooden houses that they passed while streaming toward the bridge over the Assunpink Creek that was held by Washington's main body. Under protective fire from Col. Daniel Hitchcock's Rhode Island Continental Regiment, as well as American artillery positioned below the creek, Hand and his contingent crossed over to the main line of defense behind the waterway and found Washington astride his horse beside

---

[9]Ferling, *Almost a Miracle*, 182.

[10]Fischer, 297.

the bridge, quietly watching as Cornwallis's troops pushed through the town in his direction.

It was now past 4:00 p.m., and sunset would be at 4:46 that day. Hand's regiment and the other soldiers fighting alongside it had bought Washington the time he needed to fend off the enemy because there was not enough daylight left for a full-scale assault against the American troops below the Assunpink. Cornwallis launched a series of probes to try to find a weakness in the Continental lines, but each was beaten back with heavy losses. Although Washington had fewer soldiers than his adversary, he had more artillery - with some 40 pieces to Cornwallis's 28 - and those guns were arrayed along the creek so as to provide overlapping fields of fire. The British and Hessian probes were met with "a storm of musketry, and the artillery joined in."[11] The American cannon unleashed "the heaviest fire ever delivered on any field in the Western Hemisphere up to this time."[12]

Although there is no definitive information available with regard to casualties, it has been estimated that about 365 British and Hessian soldiers were killed, wounded, or captured on 2 January as compared with approximately 100 Americans. To that extent, it may be regarded as a "great victory" for Washington and "a model of a brilliantly managed defensive battle."[13]   When darkness fell, Cornwallis called a halt to the fighting, and that evening

---

[11]Ibid., 305.

[12]Dwyer, 324.

[13]Fischer, 307.

he convened a council of war. Tradition has it that the British commander - confident that he had the Americans trapped between the creek and the Delaware River and could finish them off the next day - told his fellow officers: "We've got the Old Fox safe now. We'll go over and bag him in the morning."[14]

Unfortunately for Cornwallis, the fox would outfox the hunter, for under the cover of dark-ness, the Continentals slipped away from the creek during the early morning hours of 3 January. They embarked on a forced march that would lead to an unexpected encounter with a small British force left behind in Princeton during the advance of Cornwallis's main body to Trenton the day before, which resulted in another victory for the Americans.

To cover the movement of his forces from below the creek, Washington left behind several hundred men for part of the night with orders to keep their campfires burning "until there were several dozen veritable conflagrations blazing on the heights south of Assunpink Creek, convincing the British that the Americans were still there." He also instructed this rearguard to stay warm "by clanging picks and shovels on the frozen earth. The noise convinced British sentries that the rebels were building earthworks against tomorrow's assault."[15]

Following up their feats of daring along the Princeton Road on the afternoon of 2 January and the contribution

---

[14]Ibid., 313.

[15]Thomas Fleming, *Liberty! The American Revolution* (New York: Viking, 1997), 223.

of their lethal firepower to the success of Washington's army during its twilight stand against the enemy at the Assunpink, Col. Hand's soldiers again proved of service at Princeton the following day as they helped turn back the British charge against Gen. Nathanael Greene's division at a critical moment in the battle.

After the "Ten Crucial Days" ended, Hand's service in the Continental Army continued throughout the struggle for independence, earning him a series of promotions: to brigadier general when he was assigned to command the American troops at Fort Pitt in 1777, to brigadier general in command of a brigade of light infantry in the Marquis de Lafayette's division in 1780, to adjutant general of the army in 1781, and then to brevet major general in 1783.

Hand resigned from the military in 1783 and moved back to Lancaster, where he purchased several hundred acres of land on which he built a Georgian-style brick mansion that became known as Rock Ford Plantation. He practiced medicine and occupied a variety of civic and political positions, as a member of the Congress of Confederation (1784-1785) and the Pennsylvania Assembly (1785-1786), and as a delegate to the Pennsylvania Constitutional Convention (1790). He died of cholera in September 1802 at age 57 and was buried in St. James Episcopal Cemetery in Lancaster.

The crucial role played by Edward Hand and his riflemen in contributing to the successful outcome of the Second Battle of Trenton has been celebrated in January of every year since 1962 as part of an annual event staged by Lawrence Township, New Jersey (which Hand's men would have known as Maidenhead) to highlight its role in the Revolution. The part of the indomitable colonel has been faithfully performed by township resident William Agress on each such occasion since 1981, and he is regularly joined by other re-enactors, Revolutionary War enthusiasts, members of the Boy Scouts, township officials, and local residents. After a ceremony at the municipal building, they march south along Route 206 (which Hand's men would have known as the Princeton Road) to Notre Dame High School, adjacent to the Shabakunk Creek where Hand led the Americans in their delaying action against the enemy on 2 January 1777. Then a cannon is fired at that location to mark the occasion. Year in and year out, the remembrance of this patriot hero and the exploits of his Pennsylvania sharpshooters has no greater friend than Mr. Agress and his fellow marchers.

If any revolutionary hero deserves such a loyal following over so many years, it is surely the stout-hearted rifle commander from Lancaster. Edward Hand was "the stuff of which the hard core" of Washington's army was made.[16]

---

[16]Ketchum, 341.

Charles Scott (Paul Sawyier)

Chapter 8

Charles Scott

With weeping and with laughter
Still is the story told,
How well Horatius kept the bridge
In the brave days of old.

- Thomas Babington, Lord Macaulay, from the poem, *Horatius* in *Lays of Ancient Rome*, 1842

The 5th Virginia Continental Regiment was significantly engaged in the battles at Trenton and Princeton under the command of Col. Charles Scott, but its finest moment came while defending the stone bridge over the Assunpink Creek on 2 January, 1777. On that day, the survival of the Continental Army, and quite possibly America's quest for independence, hung in the balance.

Scott was born in Goochland County, Virginia, in 1739 and attained a rural schoolhouse education. His family traced its Virginia roots back to the mid-1600s and had once been the prosperous owner of tobacco plantations along the James River. At age 16, Scott enlisted in the 1st Virginia Regiment commanded by a 23-year-old colonel named George Washington and served as a non-commissioned officer in the ill-fated 1755 campaign against the French and their Indian allies waged by British Gen. Edward Braddock. During the French and Indian War, Washington promoted him to the rank of captain in recognition of "Scott's contributions as the finest scout, woodsman, and sergeant of the First Virginia Regiment."[1] When the conflict ended, Scott turned to farming on land bequeathed to him by his father, but he looked to re-enter military service when the Revolution broke out.

Scott raised a company of volunteers in Cumberland County in 1775 and was elected lieutenant colonel of the 2nd Virginia Regiment, which had been created by the Virginia Convention and became part of the Continental Army in February 1776. He was placed in command of the 5th Virginia Regiment on 7 May when William Peachy resigned as regimental commander. The 5th Virginia had been formed the previous February in Richmond County as the first colonial unit in the commonwealth to be established south of the James River (comprising soldiers from Bedford, Chesterfield, Hanover, Henrico, Lancaster, Loudoun, Northumberland, Richmond, Spotsylvania, and

---

[1]Tucker, 119.

Westmoreland counties). Promoted to colonel in August, Scott was reunited with his commander from the last war in November when his regiment joined up with Washington's army in New Jersey. The colonel habitually referred to Washington as "the old boss" based on his long acquaintance with the commander-in-chief, and that term of endearment "delighted his homespun 5th Virginia soldiers."[2]

In the early morning hours of 26 December 1776, Scott's regiment joined the rest of Washington's army as it marched south to Trenton through a raging northeaster to attack Col. Rall's brigade, guided by New Jersey militia from the area who knew the local topography. The 5th Virginia was assigned to the brigade commanded by Gen. Adam Stephen in Gen. Nathanael Greene's division, which joined with the brigades commanded by Gens. Hugh Mercer, William Alexander (known as Lord Stirling because he claimed the title of a Scottish earl), and de Roche Fermoy in attacking Trenton from the north and west. Scott's men were positioned on the right side of Stephen's brigade, on the strategic high ground where it provided covering fire for the advance of American forces into the center of town. Together with the three brigades in Gen. John Sullivan's division, Greene's troops caught the outnumbered and bewildered enemy in a pincer movement that won the day.

The Hessians were unable to establish a strong defensive position on the 26th because they did not take advantage of the high ground behind the Assunpink Creek, where it would have been easier to repel the American

---

[2]Ibid., 119.

assault. Washington would not make the same mistake when he brought his troops back to Trenton on the 29th and 30th and prepared for the anticipated British and Hessian counterattack; he positioned his forces behind the creek where they could most effectively fight off the enemy. Scott's regiment was part of a force dispatched by Washington halfway up the road to Princeton on New Year's Eve in order to delay any enemy movement toward Trenton. The Americans occupied a position called Eight Mile Run (known as Shipetaukin Creek today) about six miles south of Nassau Hall in Princeton, and there they skirmished with British and Hessian patrols the next day. The Continentals' stiff resistance forced the enemy to bring up reinforcements, who finally pushed the outnumbered American soldiers back but at a heavy cost. These colonials were "fighting well on good ground, holding their positions, inflicting casualties on picked troops, and taking few losses in return."[3]

When Gen. Cornwallis's column advanced down the Princeton Road toward Trenton on 2 January, Scott's 5th Virginia Regiment, along with the other units who had engaged the enemy at Eight Mile Run the day before, were waiting for them in Maidenhead. Under Col. Hand's leadership, these troops mounted a robust defense until they were forced to fall back under the weight of the enemy's superior numbers. The prolonged resistance gained Washington the time he needed to prepare for his adversary's arrival and left Cornwallis with insufficient

---

[3]Fischer, 283.

daylight to make a sustained assault on the American forces arrayed behind the Assunpink Creek.

The enemy would make three attempts to establish a foothold on the Americans' side of the Assunpink, and Scott - leading a brigade that comprised his own and two other regiments - was assigned to defend the narrow stone bridge over the creek. In Nathaniel Philbrick's estimation, "If the British managed to force their way across the bridge and overrun the American army, the war was as good as finished. . . . Washington had managed to . . . create what was, even if it is largely unappreciated today, the make-or-break moment of the War of Independence."[4] Ensign Robert Beale of the 5th Virginia reported: "Our brigade, consisting of the Fourth, Fifth and Sixth Virginia Regiments, was ordered to form in column at the bridge and George Washington came and, in the presence of us all, told Colonel Scott to defend the bridge to the last extremity. Colonel Scott answered with an oath: 'Yes, General, as long as there is a man alive.'"[5]

As his soldiers awaited the approaching enemy, Scott told them:

> *Well boys, you know the old boss has put*
> *us here to defend this bridge; and by God it*
> *must be done, let what will come. Now I want*
> *to tell you one thing. You're all in the habit of*
> *shooting too high. You waste your powder and*
> *lead, and I have cursed you about it a hundred*

---

[4]Philbrick, 82.

[5]Dwyer, 320.

times. Now I tell you what it is, nothing must be wasted, every crack must count. For that reason boys, whenever you see them fellows first begin to put their feet upon this bridge do you shin 'em. Take care now and fire low. Bring down your pieces, fire at their legs, one man Wounded in the leg is better [than] a dead one for it takes two more to carry him off and there is three gone. Leg them dam 'em I say leg them.[6]

The mettle of Scott's brigade was about to be tested by professional European soldiers who ranked among the best that the Old World could send against the New, but it appears "the old boss" knew the temper of his fellow Virginians and had good reason to repose such confidence in these soldiers. He paid them the highest compliment possible by positioning them directly behind the bridge as the Continentals' first line of defense, knowing that they would do as he had ordered, whatever the consequences.

An initial probe by British light infantry and Hessian jaegers (riflemen) reached the northern edge of the Assunpink and was beaten back. Then came a second attempt as a column of Hessian grenadiers stormed the bridge, but Scott's men and their supporting artillery (more than 20 can-non positioned in this narrow area by Gen. Knox) "shredded" the enemy advance before it could reach the middle of the bridge.[7] The grenadiers ran into "a storm of fire," with 31 killed or wounded, while 29

---

[6] Fischer, 305.

[7] Bonk, 73.

came forward to surrender "rather than retreat through the heavy fire."[8] Finally, British infantry surged forward and made their way onto the bridge, but they too were repulsed as Washington ordered Col. John Cadwalader's brigade to reinforce Scott's men.

At this point, Cornwallis pulled his forces back from the town, leaving only a couple of light infantry battalions to keep watch on the Continentals. The record of this battle was "largely missed until the accounts of many individual soldiers and junior officers on both sides emerged to document it in detail," but it was a critical part of the train of events that Americans rode to victory during the "Ten Crucial Days."[9]

Scott and his soldiers joined the other Continentals in the overnight trek to Princeton and the battle there on 3 January, followed by a three-day march to Morristown, where Washington would establish his winter quarters behind the safety of the Watchung Mountains. Scott's men would see more action that winter, even after the "Ten Crucial Days" had ended. On one such occasion, they intercepted a British foraging party near the town of Chatham and captured 70 Highlanders, in addition to "a large number of baggage wagons" that were in short supply.[10]

Col. Scott resigned his command of the 5th Virginia Regiment on 1 April 1777 and assumed the rank of

---

[8]Fischer, 305.

[9]Ibid, 307.

[10]Ibid., 352.

brigadier general the next day. As a general, he would command troops at the Battle of Germantown in October 1777, and in the last major northern engagement of the Revolutionary War during the Battle of Monmouth in June 1778, as well as the capture of the British position at Stony Point, New York in July 1779. Scott saw his last military action of the war during the British siege of Charleston, South Carolina, where he was captured when the city surrendered in May 1780. Held prisoner for two years, he was exchanged in 1782 for a British officer, Francis Lord Rawdon, and was brevetted to major general in September 1783 prior to his discharge from the Continental Army.

After the war ended, Scott moved west and settled in Woodford County, Kentucky, which was then part of Virginia. In 1788, he was selected as a member of the local board of war in his district, in charge of protecting against Indian attacks, and he led a Kentucky regiment in battle against Indian tribes from 1790 to 1794. At the same time, Scott had become active in public affairs and represented Woodford County in the Virginia General Assembly from 1789 to 1790. Kentucky became the 15th state when it was admitted to the Union in 1792, and Scott was elected its fourth governor in August 1808. He served as the state's chief executive for four years and then retired from public life. When he died in October 1813, he was buried on the grounds of his plantation, but his remains were later removed to Frankfort Cemetery in Frankfort, Kentucky.

At the time of his death, Charles Scott, at age 74, was one of the last surviving generals of the Revolutionary

War and had occupied sundry positions, both military and civilian, throughout a long and distinguished career. But the most important position that he ever held was on the ground adjacent to the stone bridge over the Assunpink Creek on 2 January 1777, at that desperate moment when the British and Hessians sought to storm across the narrow waterway separating the opposing forces in order to strike a fatal blow at Washington's army. While supported by other Continental units and militia along their flanks and rear, Scott and his Virginians were the ones who were ordered by their commander-in-chief to defend the bridge at all costs and, being nearest to it, bore the brunt of the enemy assault on that fiercely contested overpass.

When the shoot-out at the creek began, those soldiers from the Old Dominion may have held the fate of the American Revolution in their hands. And when it ended, they held the bridge.

The Deaths of Hugh Mercer (left) and John Haslet (center) at the Battle of Princeton (George Washington Parke Custis)

Chapter 9

John Haslet

The temper and character which prevail in our colonies are, I am afraid, unalterable by any human art. We cannot, I fear, falsify the pedigree of this fierce people, and persuade them that they are not sprung from a nation in whose veins the blood of freedom circulates. . . . An Englishman is the unfittest person on earth to argue another Englishman into slavery.

- Edmund Burke, Member of Parliament, from a speech to the British House of Commons *On Conciliation with America*, 22 March 1775

Col. John Haslet was a "tough, burly Irishman"[1] who commanded the 1st Delaware Continental Regiment - known as the "Delaware Blues" due to the color of their uniforms[2] - and he gave his life fighting for the independence of his adopted country at the Battle of Princeton on 3 January 1777.

---

[1]Ketchum, 233.

[2]Tucker, 262.

Haslet was about 49 years old at the time of his death and "had emerged as one of [Washington's] steadiest, most reliable officers."[3] A native of County Londonderry, Ireland, he earned a divinity degree from the University of Glasgow and was ordained a Presbyterian minister before crossing the Atlantic from Ulster in 1757 as part of a wave of Scotch-Irish immigrants seeking relief from a series of repressive measures known collectively as the Penal Laws. After settling in Pennsylvania and serving as a captain in the Pennsylvania militia during the French and Indian War, Haslet moved to Dover (Kent County), Delaware, where he practiced medicine while serving in the Delaware Assembly and operating a plantation along the Mispillion River.

Haslet would find himself serving in the ranks of the Continental Army along with many of the Scotch-Irish who had fled Ireland in search of a better life and now sought payback for the treatment accorded them under English law in their native land. For the British, the unintended consequence of this mass migration to America was that these immigrants "contributed enormously in both talent and manpower to their defeat by the Continental Army primarily made up of rebellious subjects from their colonies augmented by unforgiving former Irish victims. Haslet's participation played no small role in that outcome."[4] Indeed, about 40 percent of Washington's army consisted of Irish and Scotch-Irish soldiers, who

---

[3]Fred B. Walters, *John Haslet: A Useful One* (Fred B. Walters, 2005), vi.

[4]John Haslet. *Delaware Military History*. www.militaryheritage.org.

have been termed the "shock troops of Independence,"[5] and the "fiercest and most ardent Americans of all . . . were the Presbyterian Irish settlers and their descendants."[6]

On 19 January 1776, Haslet was given the rank of colonel and placed in command of the 1st Delaware Regiment that had been organized by the Lower Counties Assembly in Delaware in response to a call by the Continental Congress. The regiment (comprising eight companies from Kent, Sussex, and New Castle counties) was regarded as an elite entity, and its men viewed their colonel as something of a father figure.[7] There were about 750 men with Haslet's unit in the beginning, which made it the largest regiment in the army.

Haslet's regiment and William Smallwood's Maryland Continental Regiment were thought to be the "two best units in the army"[8] ; and as a history of the Maryland unit notes, "throughout most of the war, these two regiments would fight side by side."[9] The Delaware Blues, when marching on the parade ground, "had precision to match that of a veteran European unit."[10] They "were the best-drilled and probably the only completely uniformed unit in

---

[5]Tucker, 128.

[6]Ibid., 129.

[7]Ibid., 333.

[8]McCullough, *1776*, 171.

[9]Patrick K. O'Donnell, *Washington's Immortals: The Untold Story of an Elite Regiment Who Changed the Course of the Revolution* (New York: Atlantic Monthly Press, 2016), 61.

[10]Dwyer, 120.

the army. . . . and they cut quite a figure when they marched into the Perth Amboy camp [of Washington's army] in August 1776. . . . They were fiercely proud of themselves and when they went into combat they demonstrated they had every reason to be."[11]

At the Battle of Long Island on 27 August, when Gen. Howe's forces thrashed the Americans, the 1st Delaware fought beside Smallwood's regiment. Both suffered heavy losses, the Marylanders especially. They "made a desperate stand in a [plowed] field and stopped the British advance long enough for other units to get away," while an observing Washington is said to have exclaimed: "Good God! What brave fellows I must this day lose."[12] Haslet missed part of the action, having been ordered to attend the court martial of an allegedly traitorous officer in Manhattan, but he reported that his regimental colors were returned "torn with shot" from the battle.[13]

The colonel led his Delaware Blues in a successful surprise attack against a force of loyalists near the village of Mamaroneck on 22 October - a mere skirmish but a rare triumph by the Continentals while retreating from Manhattan through Westchester County - but the next day, Haslet's soldiers discovered the perils of friendly fire when they encountered a scouting party of Pennsylvania riflemen and each unit fired at the other, whom they thought to be the enemy, resulting in the death of nine

---

[11]Ketchum, 233.

[12]Fischer, 95.

[13]O'Donnell, 70.

Delaware soldiers and six riflemen. At the Battle of White Plains on the 28th, the Haslet and Smallwood regiments again fought bravely and held off Gen. Howe's troops as long as possible, yielding the enemy an unimportant victory that cost them more than twice as many casualties as those on the American side. As the retreating Americans approached the Delaware River at the beginning of December, "Washington himself marched with Haslet's Delaware men in the rear guard of the main body," and Enoch Anderson of the Delawareans reported "tearing up bridges and cutting down trees, to impede the march of the enemy."[14]

The hardships suffered by the 1st Delaware took their toll as its ranks steadily thinned throughout the summer and fall of 1776 from battlefield deaths and afflictions such as "putrid fever" (now known as typhus), smallpox, and pneumonia. By early November, only 273 of the Delaware Blues were present and fit for duty. On 22 December, only 92 were available. During the retreat of Washington's army across New Jersey in November and early December, some of the regiment "went home, with permission, to join a new regiment being formed, and some departed without permission. Nine officers left and most of their men went along with them."[15]

The enlistments of the remaining 1st Delaware soldiers expired on 30 December and all but six departed, leaving only Haslet and five others with the army - two officers,

----

[14]Fischer, 132.

[15]Dwyer, 120.

a surgeon, and two privates. The regiment was virtually extinct. Under the circumstances, Washington issued Haslet a written order to return to Delaware for the winter in order to rest and recruit new soldiers for his depleted unit, but the colonel refused to leave the army at this critical juncture. On top of this misfortune, a dubious distinction had befallen Haslet on 26 December when he tumbled into the frigid Delaware River during the crossing. As David Hackett Fischer described the mishap, "He was fished out in the nick of time, suffering much from exposure. This unconquerable man marched ten miles on severely swollen legs and fought a battle without complaint."[16]

The remnant of the 1st Delaware had been the last infantry unit to cross, having been "as-signed as the rear-guard at McConkey's Ferry, because of their discipline, toughness, and reliability."[17] Writing to his friend and fellow Delawarean, Caesar Rodney, a signatory to the Declaration of Independence, on 1 January 1777, Haslet reported: "On Christmas, at 3 o'clock we recrossed the river."[18] He led his diminished unit into combat at Trenton on 26 December, and those remaining Delaware Blues - now in the tattered remains of what had once been resplendent uniforms and shooting "from the good cover of houses, fences, and yards"- joined in providing covering fire for the charge down King Street by the 3rd Virginia Continental Regiment

---

[16]Fischer, 219. John Haslet to Caesar Rodney, January 1, 1777, in Caesar Rodney, *Letters to and from Caesar Rodney, 1756-1784*, ed. George Herbert Ryden (Philadelphia: Historical Society of Delaware, 1933), 153.

[17]Tucker, 56.

[18]Ibid., 56.

under Capt. William Washington and Lt. James Monroe.[19] Haslet's letter to Rodney expressed his frustration at not being able to do more to exploit the Trenton victory against a stunned enemy: "We should have gone on, and, panic struck, they would have fled before us, but the inclemency of the weather rendered it impossible."[20]

His limbs were still badly swollen from his accident when the Continental soldiers, after the Second Battle of Trenton, undertook their 12-mile march from the Assunpink Creek to Princeton during the early morning hours of 3 January. The determined colonel marched along beside the horse ridden by Gen. Hugh Mercer of Virginia, who was leading a brigade in Gen. Nathanael Greene's division as he had at the two engagements in Trenton, with Haslet now second in command of that unit.[21] The Americans were seeking to elude Gen. Cornwallis and possibly make a run at capturing the bounty of supplies that the British had stockpiled further north in New Brunswick.

Eager to score another victory against an enemy who suddenly appeared more vulnerable than before the events of 26 December, Haslet, in his 1 January letter to Caesar Rodney, had alluded to his swollen legs but, discounting his condition, stated: "no matter if we drive them to New York." However, he added in what may have

---

[19]Ibid., 342.

[20]Fischer, 255.

[21]Ketchum, 348.

been a premonitory note: "If I return it will be to salute you, if not we shall meet in heaven."[22]

When Washington's army reached the outskirts of Princeton, Haslet and his few men accompanied an advance guard of about 120 soldiers under Mercer as part of Greene's division. The latter formed a small left wing moving in the direction of the Princeton Road below the town while the main body under Gen. John Sullivan moved off to the right to deliver the primary attack against the enemy. Haslet advanced on foot at Mercer's side. At the same time, a British column comprised of the 17th Regiment of Foot and elements of other units under Lt. Col. Charles Mawhood was moving south to reinforce Cornwallis in Trenton. When Mawhood - "an excellent regimental commander" held "in high esteem" by Gens. Howe and Cornwallis - spotted soldiers from Greene's division, he ordered an attack.[23]

In the ensuing fight, Mercer's brigade clashed with the British in an apple orchard on the William Clarke farm and began to retreat in the face of an enemy bayonet charge. Gen. Mercer's horse was shot from under him, and he was surrounded by British soldiers. They knocked him to the ground and bayoneted him seven times when he refused their demand to surrender and instead lunged at them with his sword. (He would die of his wounds nine days later.) Haslet joined others in the brigade retreating toward the barn on the nearby Thomas Clarke farm, about half a mile

---

[22]Walters, 369

[23]Fischer, 326-327.

from the orchard. He attempted to rally those soldiers in the face of the advancing enemy, but was felled by a musket ball to the head that killed him instantly. Mercer's brigade broke and ran, but the tide of battle turned when additional American units, with Washington riding out front, came onto the battlefield and plunged into the midst of the fight, driving back the outnumbered British and forcing them to retreat into the town and the neighboring countryside in a desperate attempt to elude capture.

When the shooting ceased, the Americans had sustained some 60 to 75 casualties (killed, wounded, captured, or missing in action), most prominent among them Gen. Mercer and Col. Haslet, as compared with about 450 of Mawhood's men. Washington had chased the British out of Princeton and at that point considered a further advance toward New Brunswick with a covetous eye on the British supply depot there. He knew, however, that Cornwallis would be on the heels of his army and that the triumphant but weary Continentals were exhausted from their grueling ordeal during the prior ten days. Choosing discretion over valor, Washington headed in a northwesterly direction toward Morristown to find winter quarters for his troops.

Following Haslet's death, the Delaware Blues were reorganized under the command of David Hall (Haslet's senior captain, who was promoted to colonel), and although never again at full strength, they would see combat in Pennsylvania, New Jersey, and the southern theater. However, their fallen leader and his regiment had sacrificed as much for the cause as any unit in Washington's army. The intrepid colonel, who braved one danger after another until his luck ran out on the field at Princeton, survived long enough to help propel the army that he had so ably served into the thick of a battle that yielded the climactic victory of the "Ten Crucial Days." After Haslet died, a search of his pockets found the order that Washington had given him before the Princeton battle, to return home on a recruiting mission, which he had disregarded in order to remain with the army in its greatest hour of need.

His uniformed body was placed at Philadelphia's State House yard for an official public viewing, and he was buried in the First Presbyterian Church cemetery in Philadelphia in a casket draped with a large flag. Just two weeks after Haslet was killed, his frail wife, Jemima, "died of grief and heartache back in Delaware, never rising from her bed after receiving the tragic news of her husband's death at Princeton."[24] Caesar Rodney, writing less than a month after his friend's death, lamented his passing as follows: "We know we lost a brave, open, honest, sensible man, one who loved his country's more than his private interest."[25]

Haslet's remains would be moved to the Presbyterian Church cemetery in Dover, Delaware, in 1841, when the Delaware State Legislature voted to have a stone placed over the colonel's grave "in testimony of their respect" by a resolution "remembering his virtues as a man, his

---

[24]Tucker, 527.

[25]Walters, 381.

merit as a citizen and his services as a soldier."[26] Some 160 years after the passage of that resolution, the State of Delaware dedicated a monument to honor Haslet at Battle Monument Park in Princeton. Located near the famous Princeton Battle Monument, its inscription pays tribute to "A Patriot of considerable distinction," observing that the "distinguished service of the [1st Delaware Continental] Regiment in the campaign of 1776 can be largely attributed to his inspirational leadership" and ending with the following words: "Noted for his bravery and devotion to the cause of Liberty, Colonel John Haslet died a hero to his state and nation."[27]

Although George Washington was not generally given to public displays of emotion, legend has it that he wept over John Haslet's lifeless body on the Princeton battlefield. When the late colonel's remains were moved from Philadelphia to Dover more than six decades after his death, Philadelphia Alderman John Binns, in paying tribute to the slain hero, referred to the Delawarean's commander-in-chief as "that glorious patriot who commanded when Haslet fell and who, even in the hour of victory, watered with his tears the corpse of the gallant soldier."[28]

---

[26]Stryker, 453.

[27]The Haslet memorial is one of four small monuments located on the walkway leading to the larger Princeton Battle Monument at Battle Monument Park in Princeton. That larger monument was dedicated in 1922 by President Warren G. Harding and depicts Gen. Washington leading his troops into battle at Princeton.

[28]Walters, 7.

The Death of General Mercer at the Battle of Princeton, January 3, 1777 (John Trumbull)

Chapter 10

Joseph Moulder

A hero is no braver than an ordinary man, but he is brave five minutes longer.

- Ralph Waldo Emerson

In 1776, Joseph Moulder was a 62-year-old from Philadelphia who had made his living as a sail maker and schooner owner. As an artillery captain, he would arguably do more to win the Battle of Princeton than any other soldier in Washington's army.

Moulder served as a delegate to his colony's provincial convention in 1774 and joined the Continental Army in 1776 as the captain in command of the 2nd Company of Artillery, Philadelphia Associators. The company comprised three guns, three officers, and 82 "young men and boys" whom Moulder had recruited "from the Philadelphia waterfront: seamen, longshoremen, blockmakers, riggers, and ships' carpenters."[1] The Associators had been organized as a volunteer militia that represented a cross-section of the population in Philadelphia - then some 40,000, which made it the largest city in America at the time - as well as volunteers from rural Pennsylvania counties. They were led by Col. John Cadwalader, and one of the company commanders was the artist, Charles Willson Peale.

At the time of the British assault on Long Island in August 1776, Capt. Moulder was stationed with American forces in eastern New Jersey who were guarding against a possible enemy incursion from Staten Island across a marine channel known as the Arthur Kill. No major fighting occurred in that area during this period, but his unit became caught up in the retreat by Continental troops and militia across New Jersey into Pennsylvania following their string of defeats in New York and the ensuing British advance across the Hudson River in late November.

During the Delaware River crossing on 25 December, Moulder's Philadelphia mariners assisted the Marbleheaders in managing the boats. Moulder commanded three four-pounder guns (meaning they would have fired a four-pound ball or shell), which were among the 18 artillery pieces that the army would deploy in the First Battle of Trenton. In addition to Moulder's cannon, there were seven three-pounders, six six-pounders, and two 5.5-inch howitzers. Washington divided them equally between his two main units, with nine guns each assigned

---

[1]Fischer, 217.

to the 2nd Division under Gen. Nathanael Greene and the 1st Division under Gen. John Sullivan. Each division included about half of the 2,400 soldiers who crossed the river that night, so that this allocation of artillery to soldiers was about three times the ratio customarily employed by European armies at the time, which reflected the importance that Washington assigned to the role of artillery in this operation and more generally as well. The "possibilities, intricacies, and authority" of these big guns especially appealed to Henry Knox, who oversaw the army's use of its cannon.[2] Under his direction, the effective use of these artillery pieces, which proved "their worth as foul-weather weapons," would play a critical role in the outcome of all three battles during the "Ten Crucial Days."[3]

At Trenton on 26 December, Moulder's battery was positioned on Queen Street to fire at close range against the Hessian troops that Col. Rall was attempting to rally in a futile effort to turn back the American attack. The success of Washington's troops was due in no small measure to their decided advantage in artillery - employing 18 guns while their adversary had only six three-pounder cannon - and the fact that they were able to concentrate their pieces in a way that Rall never could because the Hessian guns were dispersed equally among his three regiments.

---

[2]Jack Kelly, *Band of Giants: The Amateur Soldiers Who Won America's Independence* (New York: Palgrave Macmillan, 2014), 57.

[3]Dwyer, 253. The author notes that at the First Battle of Trenton, many of the Americans' small arms "could not be fired because of dampened priming powder" but that the artillery was in "working order" because plugs "that had been placed in their vents and muzzles had kept them dry."

The Continentals' superiority in artillery complemented their other advantages at Trenton: the element of surprise; superior numbers, with 2,400 soldiers against 1,500 of the enemy; the state of exhaustion to which the Hessians had been reduced by having to respond to a relentless series of minor but annoying attacks by New Jersey militia during the days leading up to the battle; and the impact of the weather. The driving snow from the ongoing northeaster reduced the visibility of the Hessian defenders, as it was blowing from behind the backs of the soldiers in Greene's division into the faces of Rall's men, while the latter had to contend with dampened cartridges and firing mechanisms on their muskets from the freezing precipitation.

Contrary to what generations of Americans have believed, the Continentals enjoyed no additional advantage on 26 December from the effects of Christmas-related imbibing by the Hessians, as there is no evidence that Rall's troops engaged in any such behavior. The only drinking in Trenton that day occurred after the battle, when American soldiers discovered 40 hogsheads of rum in town, before Washington was informed and ordered that the casks be "staved in."[4]

A week later, Capt. Moulder's guns and crew were present at the Second Battle of Trenton, when Washington's army held off the British and Hessian forces under Gen. Cornwallis at the Assunpink Creek. While Moulder's battery had performed capably during the fighting at Trenton, it had not yet done anything to particularly

---

[4]Fischer, 256, and Dwyer, 271.

distinguish itself from any other unit in the army. But that was about to change.

On the march from the Assunpink to Princeton during the early morning hours of 3 January, Moulder's men and the other battery crews wrapped the wheels of their cannon in rags to deaden the sound as they circumvented the enemy on the other side of the creek. When the Continental Army arrived at the doorstep of Princeton on that frosty morning, it surprised Col. Mawhood's column of soldiers on their way to reinforce Gen. Cornwallis in Trenton.

Mawhood's unit quickly recovered from this sudden turn of events, however. Although their numbers were much less than the total American force present, the redcoats soon gained an advantage over the smaller of the two Continental divisions, that of Gen. Greene, during the confrontation on the William Clarke farm below the town. Gen. Sullivan's division was divorced from the fighting because it was moving in another direction toward the enemy force presumed to be inside the town. The British drove back Greene's men with a furious bayonet charge that struck fear into the large number of American soldiers who were not similarly equipped. When Gen. Mercer and Col. Haslet were killed, their troops fled to the rear and appeared to be on the verge of breaking apart, as efforts to organize a stand by Greene's division against the British advance floundered.

The enemy charge gave rise to what was probably the most critical juncture in this encounter, when the outcome teetered between victory and defeat. Although Mawhood's men were heavily outnumbered overall, their experience and professionalism served them well as they had clearly outfought the Americans to this point, "a testament to Mawhood's leadership and the discipline of the British Regulars."[5] It appeared that the latter were on the verge of routing Greene's battered and demoralized troops before they could be reinforced by other American units. But at this pivotal moment in both the battle and the war, Mawhood's hopes of victory were quite literally blasted by Joseph Moulder's battery.

The captain "brought his guns quickly into action. . . . [They] fired deadly rounds of grape and canister into the British infantry and stopped it."[6] The battery was stationed to the right of the Thomas Clarke house, and from there the "youthful gunners . . . made every shot tell as they mowed down the ranks of the redcoats."[7]

Moulder had only two long-barreled four-pounder cannon handled by some 20 young soldiers, but Capt. Thomas Rodney of Delaware (younger brother of John Haslet's friend, Caesar Rodney), whose militia were fighting alongside Moulder, related that the cannon were positioned where the British could not ascertain how many guns were firing at them.

As Rodney recounted,

Two pieces of artillery stood their ground and

---

[5]Fischer, 329.

[6]Ibid., 334

[7]Stryker, 284.

were served with great skill and bravery. . . .
From these stacks and buildings we . . . kept
up a continuous fire on the enemy, and in
all probability it was this circumstance that
prevented the enemy from advancing, for
they could not tell the number we had posted
behind these covers and were afraid to attempt
passing them. But if they had known how few
they were, they might easily have advanced . . .
and routed the whole body. [8]

Richard Ketchum's account of the battle echoes Thomas Rodney's analysis: "Had Mawhood realized that all that faced him . . . were two guns and perhaps a score of determined men he certainly would have ordered his troops to charge the position. . . . As it turned out, Moulder and his gunners bought the rebel army just enough time."[9]

Moulder's artillery was then joined by other guns, and more American infantry came onto the field, as the commander-in-chief urged them on: "Parade with us, my brave fellows! There is but a handful of the enemy, and we will have them directly."[10] Washington led the rallying Continentals into the center of the fight, riding to within 30 paces of the British lines. At 6 feet, two-and-a-half-inches in height, astride a white horse and wearing a uniform that clearly identified him as a general, he presented an obvious target for any enemy soldier but

------

[8]Dwyer, 345-346.

[9]Ketchum, 361.

[10]Ketchum, 361.

somehow emerged unscathed. The tide of battle quickly turned when the outnumbered British were outflanked and their line broke. They withdrew from the field with the Americans in pursuit and Washington's cry ringing in his soldiers' ears, "It is a fine fox chase, my boys!"[11]

This would prove to be one of the few major battles of the war in which Washington's army won a clear-cut victory over British troops, and the fact that it enjoyed a nearly four-to-one numerical advantage over the enemy in this engagement - at approximately 4,500 to 1,200 - was hardly incidental to the outcome.

Moulder's gunners saw further action that day. They joined a battery commanded by young Capt. Alexander Hamilton in leveling a blast at Nassau Hall, which housed the College of New Jersey and was then the largest stone building in the colonies, in order to compel the surrender of British soldiers shooting at the Americans from inside. Hamilton (who in his later role as America's first Secretary of the Treasury profoundly influenced the young republic's federal government and envisioned the development of its capitalist economy) would describe "the enterprises of Trenton and Princeton . . . as the dawnings of that bright day which afterwards broke forth with such resplendent luster."[12]

When the Continentals withdrew from Princeton to advance northward, Moulder's men had yet one more duty to perform. By their "small but important rearguard

---

[11]Ibid., 336.

[12]Ron Chernow, *Alexander Hamilton* (New York: The Penguin Press, 2004), 85.

action," these stubborn gunners helped to slow up the advance guard of light troops and mounted dragoons sent out by Cornwallis, whose force was rushing headlong from Trenton in pursuit of Washington's men. Together with 20 or more Philadelphia cavalry, Moulder's crew "discouraged the pursuers, who let the Americans go on their way."[13]

Over the next three days, Washington's soldiers made their way to the "peaceful, protected" village of Morristown. When they arrived on 6 January 1777, they found a safe haven that "could be approached by the enemy only though narrow, rugged gorges . . . [with] wood in abundance for log huts and fires, and food in the surrounding countryside." The gunners in Moulder's battery who had reached this sanctuary "were elated when one of their buddies, whom they thought they had lost at Princeton, turned up unexpectedly with a cart loaded with poultry."[14]

With this last exertion by the Continental Army, the "Ten Crucial Days" had ended and so had the fears of American soldiers and civilians alike that the demise of their cause was imminent. They now knew that the war would go on and sensed that a protracted and arduous struggle lay ahead, but one that they were more confident about winning. After all, that is what they had been doing since the night they crossed an icy river on a journey that very quickly achieved legendary status.

---

[13]Ketchum, 376.

[14]Ibid., 379.

As for the tenacious artillery officer who fended off the British charge at Princeton, he died in Philadelphia at age 65 in November 1779. "Captain Joseph Moulder does not get much space in the history books," as Richard Ketchum notes, "but it is just possible that without his services on January 3, 1777, the story of the American Revolution might have turned out rather differently."[15]

A marker graces the spot on the Princeton battlefield, now a New Jersey State Park, where an artillery battery that was led by an aging captain and manned by a score of youth from the Philadelphia waterfront once stood like a rock against an elite force of onrushing British infantry. The marker was created in 1998 by Chris Wang of Boy Scout Troop 88 of Princeton and erected by the Division of Parks and Forestry in the New Jersey Department of Environmental Protection, only a short distance from the Thomas Clarke House. (The latter requires significant restorative work if it is to continue as the last survivor of the Princeton battle, and the aficionados of this singular relic anxiously await the generosity of those with the commitment and funds to support its preservation.) Standing at the marker, an observer casts an eye on a tribute that reads in part:

> *With great skill and bravery Captain Moulder directed intense and accurate fire from the American guns which prevented the British Forces from advancing across the field. This defense was a major factor in the American victory being*

---

[15]Ibid., 360.

crucial in buying time for Washington to arrive on the field and organize a counterattack."[16]

---

[16]Site of Moulder's Battery. www.hmdb.org.

Washington at the Battle of Trenton (engraving by Illman Brothers, from a painting by Edward Henry)

Chapter 11

The View from the Riverbank

The Revolution was in the minds and hearts of the people ...

- John Adams, from a letter to Hezekiah Niles, 13 February 1818

It is an open question among some historians of the American Revolution whether the destruction of the Continental Army in the summer or fall of 1776 would have ended the war.[1] When contemplating this hypothetical scenario, Joseph Ellis acknowledged the shared optimism of John Adams and Benjamin Franklin about the ultimate triumph of the struggle for independence: "Perhaps, as [they] both ... sincerely believed, the Continental Congress would have defiantly raised another army and appointed

---

[1] Joseph J. Ellis, *Revolutionary Summer: The Birth of American Independence* (New York: Alfred A. Knopf, 2013), 185 and 208n22.

another version of Washington to lead it."[2] Nevertheless, even among those who question whether the preservation of Washington's army in 1776 was indispensable to the prospects for eventual American success, there would appear to be a consensus that the demise of that military force would, at the very least, have significantly altered the nature or course of the conflict.[3]

There is no doubt that the British had their best chance to destroy the Continental Army be-fore the events of the "Ten Crucial Days" played out. That they did not succeed in doing so may be attributed to any number of factors, as previously suggested, but is in no small part the result of the collective efforts of a determined people, many of whom have been unknown to succeeding generations of Americans. These stalwarts of the patriot cause were the "unsung heroes" of a young nation's dramatic comeback against a powerful adversary during the period from 25 December 1776 through 3 January 1777. The results achieved by its men in arms at that time were so spectacular as to rank them at the very forefront of the annals of military history by any reasonable measure of success: more than 1,700 British and Hessian soldiers killed, wounded, captured, or missing, as compared with fewer than 200 American casualties; the capture of a significant quantity of arms and supplies; and the expulsion of enemy troops from most of New Jersey. In John Ferling's vivid

---

[2] Ibid., 111.

[3] Ibid., 208n22.

phraseology, Washington's army put the enemy "through a meat grinder" during these several days of fierce combat.[4]

Although they have been largely unheralded among the general public, the "unsung" among the Continental brigades, the state militias, and other actors in our struggle for independence de-serve to be celebrated for the integral role that they played in the victories at Trenton and Princeton. They embodied the collective will that was required to achieve ultimate success in a war of attrition against a militarily superior foe.

It can be argued that the patriot cause probably owed its final success, more than anything else, to three essential facts:

First, Great Britain lacked the military capacity to conquer and control the vast expanse of territory encompassed by the colonies without more support from American loyalists than the latter were able or willing to provide.

Second, the Americans did not necessarily have to win battles to "win" the war, but only needed to persevere until Britain's willingness to expend its blood and treasure was exhausted, which is what occurred.

Third, French assistance - ranging from covert aid in the beginning of the struggle to overt intervention later on - sustained the American war effort and eventually drew Britain into a global conflict that diverted military and naval resources from its effort to subdue the American rebellion.[5]

---

[4]John Ferling, *The Ascent of George Washington: The Hidden Political Genius of an American Icon* (New York: Bloomsbury Press, 2009), 121.

[5]See chapter 25 in Ferling, *Almost a Miracle*, 562-575 and the Conclusion in

A complementary factor that relates to the preceding points is "the geographical logistics of the American continent, where every one of the . . . British [and Hessian] troops in North Ameri-ca and every bullet and every biscuit of his supply and every letter of instruction to his commanders had to be transmitted over the six-to-eight week width of the Atlantic Ocean."[6]

Even so, for the "glorious cause" to prevail, its adherents needed to sustain it for eight long years, and that required the continuing commitment of both leaders and followers. To be sure, Washington was able to preserve the Continental Army in the face of enormous recurring challenges over that period, including defeats, desertions, expired enlistments, threatened and actual mutinies, disease, and chronic shortages of equipment, food, and supplies. But he succeeded only because enough Continental soldiers and militiamen stood by the cause to deny the British outright victory and overcome the opposition of American loyalists, while prolonging the conflict long enough for American and French forces to deliver what proved to be the decisive blow to the enemy in October 1781 at Yorktown, Virginia. The colonials' dogged persistence, which often failed to win battles yet made their adversary pay dearly, reflected the steely resolve encapsulated in Nathanael Greene's memorable observation, "We fight, get beat, rise and fight again."[7]

O'Shaughnessy, 353-361

[6]Barbara W. Tuchman, *The First Salute* (New York: Alfred A. Knopf, 1988), 147.

[7]Fleming, p. 316.

Notwithstanding the primacy that generally attaches to the role of the Continental Army in winning the Revolutionary War, the contribution made by the state militias is worth noting in this context. As Larry Kidder observed in his history of a New Jersey militia regiment during the conflict, "Although Washington had little positive to say in his letters about the militia, the ways he employed it indicate he had a better opinion than he expressed outwardly, or at least he was savvy enough, or desperate enough, to bow to pragmatic necessity."[8] Also, the demarcation between the militia and the army was less clear-cut than is generally presumed, for "men moved in and out of both and men who volunteered for the Continentals were militiamen before, and frequently after, their term of enlistment, or between terms of enlistment."[9]

It belabors the obvious to suggest that the confirmation of American independence by the Treaty of Paris in September 1783 owed no less to the efforts of the rank-and-file soldier than it did to the leadership of Washington and his fellow generals. In spite of the hazards and hardships that continually afflicted the Continentals, most of them stayed the course rather than desert the cause.

Alluding to these challenges, Col. John Brooks of Massachusetts wrote to a friend from a camp near Valley Forge in 1778:

> *Under all those disadvantages no men ever*
> *shew more spirit or prudence than ours. In my*

---

[8] William L. Kidder, *A People Harassed and Exhausted: The Story of a New Jersey Militia Regiment in the American Revolution* (William L. Kidder, 2013), 12.

[9] Ibid., 10.

opinion nothing but virtue has kept our army together throughout this campaign. There has been that great principle, the love of our country, which first called us into the field, and that only to influence us.[10]

According to John Ferling:

The comradely bond that had been forged within the 'brotherhood' of soldiers was a powerful glue that held the army together. So, too, was what [Pvt. Joseph Plumb] Martin alluded to as the soldiers' 'truly patriotic' spirit. An officer, who was somewhat astonished at the soldiers' staying power in the face of baleful conditions, likewise attributed the steady service of the men to 'the principles of patriotism: they glory in the noble cause of their country.' Many among the rank and file appear to have believed with Thomas Paine that the American Revolution was about creating a new world, a place in which liberties and opportunities would surpass those that had existed in the Anglo-American world they had known before this war.[11]

The approach of the 250th anniversary of the Declaration of Independence and the epic winter of 1776-1777 will provide Americans with fresh impetus

---

[10]Commager and Morris, 649.

[11]Ferling, *Almost a Miracle*, 338.

to honor the contributions to the patriot cause made by the many unrecognized heroes who exhibited a steadfast commitment to a young nation's independence and freedom during the long revolutionary struggle. No such efforts were more important than those made in relation to the ten extraordinary days that were probably the most inspirational in the history of the United States.

That moment when America first demonstrated its national resilience speaks to us even now. If any are in doubt on that score, let them come to the banks of the Delaware River - as tens of thousands do each year from across the country and across the globe - and stand on the ground that will forever evoke images of a heroic quest for political and economic self-determination by a people who refused to be defeated in that enterprise, not even by the mightiest empire on the face of the earth. Then too, the view from the riverbank where Washington's army crossed - a bucolic setting that exudes serenity and majesty, and is free to all comers - almost conveys a spiritual sense of America's strength and the enduring quality of her democratic tradition and values.

The historical legacy of this fabled patch embodies a message that has resonated within the ranks of each generation of citizens who have met the challenges facing our republic. It began with our forefathers' spirit of self-sacrifice in the national interest and is reflected in the truth of Thomas Paine's counsel: "Those who expect to reap the blessings of Freedom must . . . undergo the fatigue of supporting it."[12]

---

[12] Paine, 147.

Appendix A

The Unsung Heroes at a Glance

	Residence	Vocation
William Blackler (1740-1818)	Massachusetts	Merchant, Shipper
Joseph Trumbull (1737-1778)	Connecticut	Merchant
Samuel Griffin (1746-1810)	Virginia	Lawyer
Mysterious Widow	New Jersey	Unknown
John Riker (1738-1794)	New York New Jersey	Physician
Joseph White (c.1755-1836)	Massachusetts	Unknown
Edward Hand (1744-1802)	Pennsylvania	Physician
Charles Scott (1739-1813)	Virginia	Farmer
John Haslet (c.1727-1777)	Delaware	Clergyman, Physician, Farmer
Joseph Moulder (1714-1779)	Pennsylvania	Sailmaker

Army Rank 1776	Military Service prior to Revolution
Captain	None
Colonel Commissary General	None
Colonel	None
Civilian	Unknown
Civilian	None
Sergeant	None
Colonel	Yes
Colonel	Yes
Colonel	Yes
Captain	Unknown

Appendix B

Chronology of Events During the "Ten Crucial Days" and the Exploits of the Unsung Heroes

14-25 December 1776

While the bulk of George Washington's army is encamped on the Pennsylvania side of the Delaware River, Continental Army soldiers and New Jersey militiamen conduct operations in the area of Mount Holly, New Jersey, engaging Hessian troops under the command of Col. Carl von Donop and monitoring their activity.

Col. Samuel Griffin leads the American forces that draw Colonel von Donop's soldiers away from their post at Bordentown to Mount Holly, where they are 18 miles from the Hessian brigade occupying Trenton under the command of Col. Johann Rall.

The mysterious widow, a beautiful young woman whose identity remains unknown, captures the attention of Col. von Donop when he stays at her home in Mount Holly and entices him to remain there long enough that his troops are too far from Trenton to assist Rall's brigade when the Continental Army attacks the latter on 26 December.

25 December 1776

The Continental Army crosses the Delaware River to assault the Hessian troops in Trenton.

Capt. William Blackler of the 14th Massachusetts Regiment, known as the Marblehead regiment, commands the boat that carries Washington across the Delaware River as part of the Marbleheaders' effort to transport the army to the New Jersey side.

The 1st Pennsylvania Regiment under **Col. Edward Hand** joins in the crossing and march to Trenton.

The 1st Delaware regiment under **Col. John Haslet** is the last American unit to cross, having been assigned as the rearguard at McConkey's Ferry. The 2nd Artillery Company, Philadelphia Associators, under **Capt. Joseph Moulder** assists the Marblehead regiment in managing the boats that carry the army across the river.

The 5th Virginia Regiment under **Col. Charles Scott** joins in the crossing and march to Trenton.

The efforts of **Commissary General Joseph Trumbull** to find food for the Continental Army prove sufficient for each soldier to receive a three-day supply of rations before crossing the river, at a time when the army is desperately short of various supplies.

26 December 1776: First Battle of Trenton

The Continental Army defeats the Hessians at Trenton to win its first significant victory of the war, then returns to Pennsylvania.

Col. Hand and his regiment join in the attack against the Hessians from the north and west of Trenton as part of the brigade commanded by Gen. Adam Stephen.

Col. Haslet and his regiment join in the attack against the Hessians from the north and west of Trenton as part of the brigade commanded by Gen. William Alexander (Lord Stirling).

Capt. Moulder commands an artillery battery that is positioned on Queen Street during the battle.

Dr. John Riker saves Lt. James Monroe's life by clamping a severed artery in his left shoulder after the young officer is wounded, along with Capt. William Washington, leading an American charge that captures a Hessian artillery battery on King Street.

Col. Scott and his regiment join in the attack against the Hessians from the north and west of Trenton as part of the brigade commanded by Gen. Matthias Alexis de Roche Fermoy.

Sgt. Joseph White joins in the charge led by Capt. Washington and Lt. Monroe to capture a Hessian artillery battery and recovers a damaged American artillery piece that he and several others bring back across the Delaware River after the battle.

29-30 December 1776

The Continental Army returns to Trenton, and Washington's troops combine with militia from Pennsylvania and New England to form a consolidated force that entrenches itself below the Assunpink Creek.

31 December 1776

Col. Scott and his regiment join other units skirmishing against the enemy along the Princeton Road in Maidenhead (Lawrence Township today).

2 January 1777: Second Battle of Trenton

The Continental Army holds off an attack by British and Hessian forces along the Assunpink Creek.

Col. Hand leads his regiment and other units, including the regiment under **Col. Scott**, in fighting a delaying action against British and Hessian troops under Gen. Charles Cornwallis in Maidenhead, and by so doing slows Cornwallis's march to Trenton long enough to prevent him from launching a full-scale, coordinated assault in daylight against Washington's army arrayed behind the Assunpink Creek.

Capt. Moulder commands an artillery battery that joins in the barrage by American cannon along the southern bank of the creek against the advancing British and Hessian troops.

Col. Scott commands a brigade that holds the bridge over the Assunpink Creek and beats back a series of probing actions by British and Hessian troops, with support from other Continental units.

3 January 1777: Battle of Princeton

The Continental Army marches 12 miles overnight from behind the Assunpink Creek to Princeton and defeats the British force stationed there for the capstone American victory of the "Ten Crucial Days."

Col. Haslet joins in the march and battle while hobbled by swollen limbs from falling into the Delaware River on the 26 December return crossing. He is killed while attempting to rally the American soldiers in Gen. Nathanael Greene's division against the charge of British troops commanded by Lt. Col. Charles Mawhood.

Capt. Moulder commands an artillery battery that halts the British advance at a pivotal moment, long enough for other American troops to arrive on the field and turn the tide of battle.

Col. Hand and his regiment join in the effort to turn back the British charge.

Sgt. White commands an artillery piece during the battle.

3-6 January 1777:

The Continental Army makes its way from Princeton to Morristown, where it establishes its winter quarters and thereby ends the military campaign associated with the "Ten Crucial Days."

Bibliography

Books

Bonk, David. *Trenton and Princeton 1776-77: Washington Crosses the Delaware.* New York: Osprey Publishing, 2009.

Brookhiser, Richard. *Founding Father: Rediscovering George Washington.* New York: The Free Press, 1996.

Bunker, Nick. *An Empire on the Edge: How Britain Came to Fight America.* New York: Alfred A. Knopf, 2014.

Chernow, Ron. *Alexander Hamilton.* New York: The Penguin Press, 2004.

Chernow, Ron. *Washington: A Life.* New York: The Penguin Press, 2010.

Commager, Henry Steele, and Richard B. Morris, eds. *The Spirit of 'Seventy-Six: The Story of the American Revolution as Told by Participants.* New York: Harper & Row, Publishers, 1967.

Dale, Frank. *Delaware Diary: Episodes in the Life of a River.* New Brunswick, NJ: Rutgers University Press, 1996.

Dwyer, William M. *The Day Is Ours!: November 1776 - January 1777: An Inside View of the Battles of Trenton and Princeton.* New York: The Viking Press, 1983.

Ellis, Joseph J. *Revolutionary Summer: The Birth of American Independence.* New York: Alfred A. Knopf, 2013.

Faragher, John Mack. *The Encyclopedia of Colonial and Revolutionary America.* New York: Da Capo Press, 1996.

Ferling, John. *Almost a Miracle: The American Victory in the War of Independence.* New York: Oxford University Press, 2007.

Ferling, John. *The Ascent of George Washington: The Hidden Political Genius of an American Icon.* New York: Bloomsbury Press, 2009.

Ferling, John. *Whirlwind: The American Revolution and the War That Won It.* New York: Bloomsbury Press, 2015.

Fischer, David Hackett. *Washington's Crossing*. New York: Oxford University Press, 2004.

Fleming, Thomas. *Liberty! The American Revolution*. New York: Viking, 1997.

Glickstein, Don. *After Yorktown: The Final Struggle for American Independence*. Yardley, PA: Westholme Publishing, LLC, 2015.

Kelly, Jack. *Band of Giants: The Amateur Soldiers Who Won America's Independence*. New York: Palgrave Macmillan, 2014.

Ketchum, Richard M. *The Winter Soldiers*. Garden City, NY: Doubleday & Company, Inc., 1973.

Kidder, William L. *A People Harassed and Exhausted: The Story of a New Jersey Militia Regiment in the American Revolution*. William L. Kidder, 2013.

McCullough, David. *John Adams*. New York: Simon & Schuster, 2001.

McCullough, David. *1776*. New York: Simon & Schuster, 2005.

McDowell, Bart. *The Revolutionary War*. Washington, DC: National Geographic Society, 1967.

Middlekauff, Robert. *The Glorious Cause: The American Revolution, 1763-1789*. New York: Oxford University Press, 2005.

Middlekauff, Robert. *Washington's Revolution: The Making of America's First Leader*. New York: Alfred A. Knopf, 2015.

Monroe, James. *The Autobiography of James Monroe*. Edited and with an introduction by Stuart Gerry Brown. Syracuse, NY: Syracuse University Press, 1959.

Nelson, Eric. *The Royalist Revolution: Monarchy and the American Founding*. Cambridge, MA: The Belknap Press of Harvard University Press, 2014.

O'Donnell, Patrick K. *Washington's Immortals: The Untold Story of an Elite Regiment Who Changed the Course of the Revolution.* New York: Atlantic Monthly Press, 2016.

O'Shaughnessy, Andrew Jackson. *The Men Who Lost America: British Leadership, the American Revolution, and the Fate of the Empire.* New Haven, CT: Yale University Press, 2013.

Osborne, Peter. *No Spot In This Far Land Is More Immortalized: A History of Pennsylvania's Washington Crossing Historic Park.* Yardley, PA: Yardley Press, 2014.

Paine, Thomas. *Collected Writings.* New York: The Library of America, 1955.

Philbrick, Nathaniel. *Valiant Ambition: George Washington, Benedict Arnold, and the Fate of the American Revolution.* New York: Viking, 2016.

Rodney, Caesar. *Letters to and from Caesar Rodney, 1756-1784.* ed. George Herbert Ryden, Philadelphia; Historical Society of Delaware, 1933.

Stryker, William S. *The Battles of Trenton and Princeton.* Boston: Houghton, Mifflin and Company, 1898.

Tuchman, Barbara W. *The First Salute.* New York: Alfred A. Knopf, 1988.

Tucker, Phillip Thomas. *George Washington's Surprise Attack: A New Look at the Battle That Decided the Fate of America.* New York: Skyhorse Publishing, 2014.

Walters, Fred B. *John Haslet: A Useful One.* Fred B. Walters, 2005.

Wickes, Stephen. *History of Medicine in New Jersey.* Newark, NJ: Martin R. Dennis & Co., 1879.

Wiencek, Henry. *An Imperfect God: George Washington, His Slaves, and the Creation of America.* New York: Farrar, Straus and Giroux, 2003.

Wood, Gordon S. *Revolutionary Characters: What Made the Founders Different.* New York: The Penguin Press, 2006.

Online Sources

The following websites were accessed during the period from November 2015 to April 2016:

Bell, J. L. *Joseph White: good speller, sickly soldier. Boston 1775*, 18 July 2006. www.boston1775.blogspot.com.

Brigadier General Edward Hand. National Park Service: Yorktown Battlefield. www.nps.gov.

Britton, Rick. James Monroe: Bona Fide Hero of the American Revolution. *Journal of the American Revolution Online Magazine*, 31 January 2013. www.allthingsliberty.com.

Captain William Blackler (1740-1818). www.ashefamily.info.

Clark, Ellen McCallister, and Emily L. Schulz. *Delaware in the American Revolution: An Exhibition from the Library and Museum Collections of The Society of the Cincinnati, Anderson House, Washington, D.C.*, October 12, 2002 - May 3, 2003. The Society of the Cincinnati, 2002. www.societyofthecincinnati.org.

Col Samuel Griffin. www.findagrave.com.

Deborah Sampson (1760-1827). National Women's History Museum.www.nwhm.org/education-resources/biography/biographies/deborah-sampson.

Dr. John Riker. www.zoominfo.com.

Edward Hand Papers. Historical Society of Pennsylvania. www.hsp.org.

5th Virginia Regiment (Revolutionary War). www.familysearch.org.

Gardner, Frank A. Glover's Marblehead Regiment in the "*War of the Revolution*". *Massachusetts Magazine*, I:2, April 1908. www.archive.org.

General Charles Scott. www.rootsweb.ancestry.com.

Gianakon, Julie. *Doctor Riker's decision.* Hektoen International, Spring 2014. www.hektoeninternational.org.

Ippolito, Steven Christopher. *George Washington and James Monroe: Military, Political, and Diplomatic Relations 1776-1799.* www.militaryhistoryonline.com.

Jacob Francis, 1754–1836, African American. Crossroads of the American Revolution National Heritage Area. www.revolutionarynj.org.

John Haslet. Delaware Military History. www.militaryheritage.org.

Joseph Moulder. www.geni.com.

Kentucky Governor Charles Scott. Governors/Former Governors' Bios, National Governors Association. www.nga.org.

Kraft, Randy. "Crossroads At The Crossing: Turnaround Begins In Small Steps At Historic Park". *The Morning Call,* 25 December 1994. http://articles.mcall.com.

PlanetPrinceton. *53rd Annual Colonel Hand March in Lawrenceville: January 3, 2015 @ 10:00 am - 2:00 pm.* www.planetprinceton.com.

Robinson, Karina. *Francis, Jacob (1754-1836).* www.blackpast.org.

Schenawolf, Harry. *Battle of Mamaroneck, New York "A Pretty Affair."* Shades of Liberty: Josiah. www.harryschenawolf.com.

Site of Moulder's Battery. www.hmdb.org.

Talbott, Tim. *Veterans of the American Revolution Elected Governor.* ExploreKYHistory. http://explorekyhistory.ky.gov.

The Shot Heard Round the Word: The Battles of Lexington and Concord: "Concord Hymn" - Ralph Waldo Emerson. www.

constitutionfacts.com.

Trumbull, Joseph, (1737-1778). *Biographical Directory of the United States Congress, 1774-Present.* http://bioguide. congress.gov.

Van Winkle Keller, Kate. *Joseph White: A Biographical Note and Preliminary Checklist of his Publications, 1783-1833.* American Antiquarian Society, 2008. www. americanantiquarian.org.

Welborn, Dr. Cliff. *Supply Line Warfare. Army Logistician*, 40:6, November-December 2008. www.almc.army.mil.

Unpublished Material

Heinemann, Heinz J. *The Weather when Washington crossed the Delaware.* Unpublished report. *Washington Crossing*, PA: Washington Crossing Historic Park. Pennsylvania Historical and Museum Commission, October 2001.

Winter 2015 Program Book: 2015 Annual Reenactment of Washington Crossing the Delaware River. Washington Crossing, PA: Washington Crossing Historic Park. Pennsylvania Historical and Museum Commission and the Friends of Washington Crossing Park.

Acknowledgments

The reader is advised that, notwithstanding my current status as a historical interpreter at Washington Crossing Historic Park and the fact that I conduct guided tours there on behalf of the Friends of Washington Crossing Park, I am speaking in these pages for myself only. The views expressed in this narrative are mine alone, except insofar as they may be specifically attributed to another author or historical account, and do not represent those of WCHP staff or the Friends group. Although I wish to gratefully acknowledge the assistance provided by others in connection with this work, I bear sole responsibility for its content.

While at WCHP, I have had the opportunity to work with the Friends group in a variety of ways and over many hours, in particular leading tours of the lower park and assisting at special events throughout the year, including the renowned annual re-enactment of the crossing on Christmas day and the not-quite-as-famous "dress rehearsal" for the annual re-enactment that is held on the second Sunday in December.

During this time, I have come to know many volunteers and staff with the Friends group and to appreciate their knowledge, dedication, and willingness to share information about all manner of subjects relating to the "Ten Crucial Days" and other aspects of the Revolutionary War and life in Colonial America. I am grateful to all these individuals, but especially to Tom Maddock, Pat Seabright, and Bob Whalen for "showing me the ropes" when I was learning how to be an interpreter at the park, and to Bunkie Maddock for planting the seed from which the idea to pursue this project germinated. I am particularly indebted to Tom, Pat, and Bunkie, along with Judi Biederman, for reviewing and commenting on a draft of this work.

In addition, this project has greatly benefited from the generous assistance provided by my extended family members: Linda Lehans contributed her rigorous editorial efforts, and

Phillip Lehans shared his insights about cover design issues. I owe them big time.

Thanks are particularly due to Roger Williams and Vince Rospond for working their publishing magic at Knox Press, and to Roger for his insights relating to vexillology (the study of flags) and Revolutionary War literature, as well as for giving a splendid tour of the Princeton battlefield to volunteers and staff with the Friends group.

Dianne Breen at WCHP deserves a shout-out for sharing helpful sources of information and assisting in my collection of related artifacts. Joe Capone, the executive director of the Friends group, assistant director Jennifer Martin, and WCHP bookstore coordinator Connie Unangst have all been supportive as well, and for that I am most appreciative.

I am also obliged to Kathie Ludwig, Librarian at the David Library of the American Revolution, whose assistance reinforced my sense of that institution's immense value as a resource for anyone seeking information about virtually anything relating to our nation's struggle for independence.

Of course, people who do what I do at WCHP are beholden to the authors whose titles have left us such a rich historical record to draw from in our study and discussion of the "Ten Crucial Days," and that indebtedness has become even more readily obvious to me as a result of this undertaking.

Most especially, I would like to thank my wife Alison for enduring my many foibles and sharing the interest in early America that prompted me to undertake this effort, but then I should probably expect no less from someone who (I am told and have no reason to doubt) is descended from a passenger on the *Mayflower* and whose favorite football team is named the "Patriots."

Finally, I need to acknowledge the current and recent custodians of WCHP - the Pennsylvania Department of Conservation and Natural Resources and the Pennsylvania

Historical and Museum Commission, respectively - and above all the park itself. Being there has provided me with a welcome outlet for a long-standing and passionate interest in the Revolutionary War era, and I have thoroughly enjoyed the opportunity to share that passion with visitors of varying ages, backgrounds, and nationalities. My time there has also yielded a deeper appreciation of how the historical legacy of this beloved, legendary venue touches people who journey from down the street and across the ocean; and when I see visitors from distant lands come to WCHP, as I often do, I think it must be because its hallowed ground represents the best of what our country is about—a beacon of freedom and hope to so many people in so many places. It is a reminder that Thomas Paine's words still ring true today: "The cause of America is in a great measure the cause of all mankind."

Index

A Note About the Author

David Price is a historical interpreter at Washington Crossing Historic Park in Pennsylvania. Under the auspices of the Friends of Washington Crossing Park, he conducts guided interpretive tours at this Registered National Historic Landmark and site of the Continental Army's crossing of the Delaware River in 1776, focusing on the "Ten Crucial Days" of the American Revolution and other historical aspects of the park. He holds degrees in political science from Drew University and Rutgers University - New Brunswick, and was a nonpartisan research analyst with the New Jersey Legislature for 31 years. A member of the Crossroads of the American Revolution Association, the Museum of the American Revolution, the Old Barracks Association, and the Princeton Battlefield Society, he lives very near the route traversed by Revolutionary War soldiers through Maidenhead Township in New Jersey, known today as Lawrence Township. The latter was so named in 1816 to honor Captain James Lawrence, a naval hero of the War of 1812 whose dying words are among the most celebrated in American military history: "Don't give up the ship!"

Additional books on the "Ten Crucial Days"

David Hackett Fischer
Washington's Crossing

William L. (Larry) Kidder
*A People Harassed and Exhausted: The Story of a New
Jersey Militia Regiment in the American Revolution*

Crossroads of the Revolution: Trenton, 1774-1783

*Ten Crucial Days: Washington's Vision for Victory
Unfolds*

*Revolutionary Princeton- 1774-1783: The Biography
of an American Town in the Heart of a Civil War*

*The Revolutionary World of a Free Black Man: Jacob
Francis 1754-1836*

Mark Maloy
*Victory or Death: The Battles of Trenton and
Princeton, December 25, 1776—January 3, 1777*

David Bonk
*Trenton and Princeton 1776-77: Washington Crosses
the Delaware*

Relive the "Ten Crucial Days" of the American Revolution

Washington Crossing Historic Park

This Pennsylvania state park and National Historic Landmark is where the Continental Army embarked on its epic crossing of the Delaware River on December 25-26, 1776, which may have saved our nation's quest for independence when the American Revolution appeared all but lost. The park offers more than 500 acres of American history, natural beauty, and family fun.

Washington Crossing State Park

This New Jersey state park lies opposite its sister park on the Pennsylvania side and is part of the same National Historic Landmark area. It is the site where the Continental Army landed after crossing the Delaware River to attack the Hessian brigade occupying Trenton. In addition to its historical significance, the 3,500-acre park is well known for its trails and wildlife habitat.

Old Barracks Museum

This museum in Trenton has a unique history dating back to 1758, when it was built to house British soldiers during the French and Indian War. It was occupied by Hessian soldiers when the Continental Army attacked on December 26, 1776. From military quarters to widow's home, from brothel to museum, the building offers visitors a fascinating look at the history of the area.

Princeton Battlefield

This New Jersey state park is where the Battle of Princeton was fought on January 3, 1777 - the capstone event of the "Ten Crucial Days" campaign that altered the course of the war. It is the site of what is considered to be the fiercest fight of its size during the long conflict. The 1772 Clarke House witnessed the battle and served as sanctuary for General Hugh Mercer, who died there nine days later; it contains period furniture and Revolutionary War exhibits.

Learn more about these historic sites at:
www.tencrucialdays.org